how to

D1102372

ABOUT THE AUTHORS:

Chris Nelson founded *Freeride* – the UK's cult surf, skate, snowboard publication – and spent six years hitting the world's top events and interviewing surfing's heroes and anti-heroes. He has also contributed to some of the UK's most respected boarding publications.

Demi Taylor headed up the UK communications for one of the world's largest boardsports companies and is a surf/travel photo-journalist. They are both committed surfers and in 2001 took the ultimate road-trip, surfing Europe from the northern tip of Scotland to the desert south of Morocco.

Despite their travels, Chris's favourite break, a reef, can be found on England's north-east coast, while Demi favours surfing with the seals in a bay on Scotland's North Shore

how to be a
surfer

chris nelson
& demi taylor

**Illustrations by
Zac Sandler**

PUFFIN BOOKS

PUFFIN BOOKS

Published by the Penguin Group
Penguin Books Ltd, 80 Strand, London WC2R 0RL, England
Penguin Putnam Inc., 375 Hudson Street, New York, New York 10014, USA
Penguin Books Australia Ltd, 250 Camberwell Road, Camberwell, Victoria 3124, Australia
Penguin Books Canada Ltd, 10 Alcorn Avenue, Toronto, Ontario, Canada M4V 3B2
Penguin Books India (P) Ltd, 11 Community Centre, Panchsheel Park, New Delhi – 110 017, India
Penguin Books (NZ) Ltd, Cnr Rosedale and Airborne Roads, Albany, Auckland, New Zealand
Penguin Books (South Africa) (Pty) Ltd, 24 Sturdee Avenue, Rosebank 2196, South Africa

Penguin Books Ltd, Registered Offices: 80 Strand, London WC2R 0RL, England

www.penguin.com

First published 2003
3

Text copyright © Chris Nelson and Demi Taylor 2003
Illustrations copyright © Zac Sandler 2003
All rights reserved

The moral right of the authors and illustrator has been asserted

Set in Helvetica

Made and printed in England by Clays Ltd, St Ives plc

British Library Cataloguing in Publication Data
A CIP catalogue record for this book is available from the British Library

ISBN 0–141–31624–1

PUBLISHER'S NOTE

Outdoor recreational activities are, by their very nature, potentially hazardous. All participants in
such activities must assume responsibility for their own actions and safety. If you have any
health problems or medical conditions, consult your doctor before undertaking any outdoor
activities. The information contained in this guidebook cannot replace sound judgement and
good decision-making, which can help reduce risk exposure, nor does the scope of this book
allow for disclosure of all the potential hazards and risks involved in such activities. Learn as
much as possible about the outdoor recreational activities in which you participate, prepare for
the unexpected and be cautious. The reward will be a safer and more enjoyable experience.

Maisie, Bronwen and Richard
– thank you for helping us focus on the horizon

*And thanks to all the surfers who gave up time in the
water to share some advice with tomorrow's boardriders!*

contents

1
Only a surfer knows the feeling

'I'm not a great surfer but nothing feels quite as good as paddling out into the ocean on a surfboard and sitting there with the swell and the rhythm of the ocean ... for anyone out there who's thinking about trying it, just do it. It's great for you and it makes you feel real good.'
Anthony Kiedis – lead singer of Red Hot Chilli Peppers

The sun is shining and the crystal-clear blue waves are fanned by a light offshore breeze. You see a four-foot set approaching and, as if in slow motion, you turn and paddle. As the wave begins to take you, you pop to your feet in a fluid motion. Your board glides out on to the open face. You stretch out your arm, trailing your fingers in the glassy wall. You can just about hear your mates hooting in the background. As time speeds up with you, you accelerate down the face of the wave. You feel as if you are flying, your heart is racing as the power of the wave carries you on. When the ride finishes, you're shaking all over with excitement and the rush of adrenalin. Although your arms and legs have turned to jelly, you paddle back out into the line-up with new energy, eager to re-live that moment again and again. A cold winter of watching surf movies and reading surf mags cover to cover has given way to an endless summer of wave riding.

So, how do you become a surfer? And what is a surfer? Is it all about learning to stand up on a board or is there a bit more to it than that?

Being a surfer takes more than just walking around with a board under your arm and talking like Keanu Reeves in *Point Break*. As Pappas, his FBI partner in the film points out, **'To become a surfer you gotta get out there in the water. These guys are like a tribe, they've got their own way of speaking, own way of dressing ...'**

Being a surfer means you know when the swell's coming and where it's going to hit. The difference between a beach break and a point break. Why we want a wave to peel and not close out. And why we're going right when the rest of the world think we're going left!

Surfing is like a huge puzzle. On their own the pieces don't mean very much but put them together and the whole scene is revealed. This book will give you all the pieces to the puzzle but to see the bigger picture you will need perseverance, dedication and staying power. Some days you'll have got up at dawn and it's flat or it will be howling with wind or freezing cold or you simply can't get a lift to the beach. But then on other days the sun will be shining, the swell will be pumping and you'll be out there, sharing the waves, the stoke and the stories with your mates.

2
Surfing's colourful history

Back in the 1950s, admitting to your parents that you were a surfer would have been the equivalent of telling them you had sold your granny and joined the Hell's Angels. Surfers, with their 'don't care' attitude and secret language, were the original rebels – every parent's nightmare. But if you hit the beach this weekend you'll probably see whole generations of families taking to the water. So what has changed since board riding's rebellious beginnings?

Sport of kings

Forget grouse shooting or falconry, there is only one original sport of kings – and that's surfing. When famous British explorer Captain Cook arrived in Hawaii in the 1770s, he was met by an amazing sight. The Hawaiians were walking on water! Well, as the first westerner ever to see someone surfing that's how it must have appeared. Surfing was all about status – the more important you were, the bigger your board, and royalty rode boards up to 16ft in length (that's two cars parked nose to nose). It was also a good way to get a date. All you had to do was to jump on to the board of the person you fancied and ride a wave together to the beach.

Unfortunately boards are a lot smaller these days!

The arrival of westerners in Hawaii did for surfing what the Ice Age did for sunbathing. Missionaries soon banned wave riding, probably because they considered anything this much fun to be the work of the devil!

It was about 100 years before surfing hit the headlines again. **Duke Kahanamoku** ('The Duke') was probably surfing's most important personality. A Waikiki Beach boy, Olympic gold medallist swimmer and surfing's ultimate promoter, he travelled the globe showcasing the sport and sowing the seeds for the subsequent surf explosion. But modern surfing is a million miles away from the original sport of kings. In those days, surfers rode straight towards the beach rather than across the face of the wave. The boards were fin-less and made of solid, heavy redwood. In fact you had to be built like the Hulk just to carry your board down the beach.

Surfing reaches the mainland

In the 1930s, a Californian named **Tom Blake** was frustrated with riding in one direction, so he built a lighter, hollow board and added a fin to the bottom, so he could turn and surf across the face of the wave. About the same time, a polystyrene-type wood, balsa, was discovered. This meant that boards were now light enough for everyone to have a go.

Gidgets, fins and aeroplane wings – surfing takes over the world

The 1950's surf scene grew up around Malibu Point on the West Coast of America before evolving into what became known as the 'Malibu Era'. Some surfers spent

the war working in aircraft design so when they went back to the beach, they took this technology with them. Foam and fibreglass revolutionised the way boards were built, and are still used to this day. These lighter boards, known as Malibus, were more manoeuvrable, enabling a new way of riding. They allowed riders to 'walk the board', 'hang ten' and 'drop-knee turn'.

This was an era ruled by Californians **Mickey Dora** and **Phil Edwards**, who helped pioneer surfing on Hawaii's North Shore, with Edwards becoming the first man ever to ride Hawaii's infamous Pipeline. Dora was to surfing what the Gallaghers are to music – highly talented with a blatant disregard for authority. Known as 'Da Cat' for his uncanny style in the water, this Malibu local was the ultimate anti-hero for his generation and beyond. But it wasn't just the guys taking on the Hawaiian waves. Fifteen-year-old **Linda Benson** was about to become the youngest competitor to win the Makaha International and the first woman ever to surf awesome big-wave spot Waimea.

If you weren't a surfer, you didn't understand them. The way they talked, the way they dressed, the way they lived their lives – hanging on the beach by day and partying by night. The Second World War had just finished and as the ultimate act of rebellion, some even took to wearing German army helmets in the line-up. But surfers weren't bad; they were just the original rebels.

Then a young girl called **Kathy Kohner** decided she wanted to learn to surf. The other surfers at Malibu nicknamed her **Gidget**, the Girl Midget, and her father, a Hollywood writer, made the eponymous film. Suddenly surfing was the coolest thing on the planet and surf mania exploded.

The Sixties saw a whole line of Hollywood films, mainly love stories or musicals set at the beach with surfing heroes and heroines. During this decade of massive social change, The Beach Boys brought the surf sound into everyone's home and *The Endless Summer* was the first true surf film to go on national release. Everyone wanted to be a surfer!

Chasing the curl

In the late Sixties **George Greenough** and fellow Australian **Nat Young** came up with a revolutionary, short, manoeuvrable board which made it possible to surf near 'the curl' – the breaking part of the wave. In 1966, Nat won the World Championships on one of these radical new boards, pioneering the shortboard revolution. Overnight, people literally cut 2ft off their Malibus.

Meanwhile in Hawaii the first Duke Kahanamoku Invitational Competition was taking place at Sunset Beach, the legendary big wave spot. Seventeen-year-old **Jeff Hakman** earned himself the title 'Mr Sunset' and universal respect, winning this prestigious event.

By the Seventies boards had dropped in size to between 6 and 7ft and had begun to look more like modern shortboards. In the late Seventies **Mark Richards** pioneered the 'twin-fin', a board with two fins instead of one for extra manoeuvrability. Known as 'The Wounded Seagull' for his unique surf style, he went on to become the first surfer to win the World Title four times in a row (only bettered by **Kelly Slater** nearly 20 years later). In 1981 pro surfer **Simon Anderson** claimed three back-to-back contest victories and changed the face of modern surfing forever with a radical new design. His three-finned board, the 'Thruster', gave the rider even more manoeuvrability and greater control in all surfing conditions and is still what the majority of surfers are riding today.

The modern era

In the 1980s competitive surfing took off with an era dominated by legends **Tom Carroll**, **Tom Curren**, **Occy**, **Damian Hardman** and ultimate power surfer **Gary Elkerton**. 100,000 people packed Huntington Beach for the OP Pro and big money deals were signed by the top riders. 1983/84 World Champion, Tom Carroll became surfing's first million-dollar man and with 26 tour victories under his belt became one of the most influential surfers of the 80s and 90s. On the flip side of the coin was Tom Curren. Despite becoming a three-time World Champion and being universally regarded as the sport's smoothest surfer, he has continued to shy away from the spotlight, remaining a true soul surfer at heart and an inspiration to a new breed of free surfers.

New skool

By the early Nineties surfboards had become smaller and lighter as progressive surfers like **Christian Fletcher** and **Martin Potter** brought moves like the aerial from the skate ramp into the water. The 'new skool' was born. Fletcher came from a true surfing family that included his five times World Championship winning aunt, **Joyce Hoffman**. Although English-born Potter and his family moved to wave-rich South Africa, he didn't start surfing until he was 13. However, two years later, with a freakish natural talent he hit the world circuit and never looked back. In 1989 'Pottz' became the first British World Champion and influenced a whole generation of surfers with his new style of surfing.

Soon after, a young Floridian surfer by the name of Kelly Slater emerged on to the scene. The likes of Slater, **Rob Machado** and **Shane Herring** were pioneers of this new movement, riding 'banana boards' – thin boards with lots of nose and tail 'rocker'. Their speedy, snappy surfing in small waves and skateboard-inspired 'tailslides' and '360s' did not appeal to all, but changed the face of modern surfing. Slater was now the best surfer on the planet and backed by the biggest surf company (Quiksilver) in the world. He won an unprece-dented six World Titles before retiring in 1998 to con-centrate on free surfing.

But it wasn't just the men making waves. In 1997 **Lisa Andersen** brought women's surfing into a new era of professionalism and claimed her fourth consecu-tive world title. Women's surfing has always had a tradi-tion of producing strong and consistent performers. America's **Margo Oberg** and **Freida Zamba** and South African-born **Wendy Botha** are all four-times World Champions, while **Layne Beachley** is a five-time Champion.

The unridden realm

Big-wave surfing – taking on waves as big as houses – grew to become front-page news around the world in the mid-Nineties. New breaks like Mavericks and Todos Santos hit the headlines and the deaths of three riders in big surf rocked the sport. In 1998 K2 sponsored an event to find the biggest wave paddled into and ridden

that year. A competition surfer, **Taylor Knox**, not previously known for big-wave exploits, took the $50,000 first prize when he took off on a wave with a 50ft face, about the size of four double-decker buses, during the Reef Big-Wave competition at Todos Santos. It is regarded as the biggest wave ever ridden by non 'tow-in' means.

The ASP tour

Such is the popularity of competitive surfing, the Association of Surfing Professionals or ASP, (the sport's governing body) now has two tours. The WCT (World Championship Tour) is the equivalent of Formula One, with events held around the world throughout the year. The WQS is the qualifying series for all aspiring pros' and events take place around the globe. Just like football leagues, at the end of each year surfers are promoted and demoted between the tours depending on their performances. This millennium a new order has emerged, which is headed by 2001 World Champion **CJ Hobgood** and brother **Damien**, and includes **Shea** and **Cory Lopez** and **Andy Irons**. Along with **Taj Burrows**, **Joel Parkinson** and **Mick Fanning** these guys are seen as the future of the contest scene, but first they will have to deal with Kelly Slater – fresh out of retirement in 2002.

The future

Away from contest surfing, a group of watermen from Maui, headed by **Laird Hamilton**, were busy experimenting like mad scientists. They found a way to surf waves that were too big to paddle into. They used jet-skis to tow each other into 50ft waves on boards with foot-straps. The team, including **Darrick Doerner**,

Pete Cabrinha and **Buzzy Kerbox**, pioneered a break called Jaws on Maui, surfing the biggest waves ever ridden at the time.

Tow-in surfing is now used by many top surfers including **Mike Parsons**, **Peter Mel** and Layne Beachley who is a regular tow-in rider with her partner **Ken Bradshaw**. Ken is credited with riding the biggest wave ever when he was towed into a 60ft-plus face outside Log Cabins. How long this record lasts depends on the size of the next swell to hit Hawaii. The riders are ready to go at a day's notice.

Just imagine riding a wave tall as four double-decker buses!

3
Technique

When you look out on perfect hollow waves and see a surfer casually tuck under the lip and into the barrel, it's amazing how easy they make it all seem. But one thing you need to remember is that everyone has to start somewhere, usually floundering about in the white water. **'When we started in Newcastle, I think for the first three years we didn't get out of the white water pretty much,'** says **Sam Lamiroy**, now one of the UK's top pro surfers. At this stage in your surfing evolution you must concentrate on one thing and that's having fun – because you certainly won't look cool!

The reason surfing is so rewarding is because it's so difficult to learn. **'It's not until you get on a board that you realize you can't even lie on it, paddle it, sit on it, anything,'** says top British female surfer **Sarah Bentley**. **'And to make it even worse, you lie on your board and try to paddle it out and there are these waves that keep crashing at you and you think, *Hang on, if these waves stopped I could actually get this board out back and then it would be OK.'*** However, soon things will be getting easier. **'Every time you go in, you get a little bit more capable. Maybe it's a psychological thing or maybe your body is getting more used to it or maybe you're just more determined,'** explains Sarah.

As four times World Champion Lisa Andersen explains, just because it's difficult, it doesn't mean it isn't fun. **'Surfing is a hard sport to learn. It took a lot of trial and error but I just kept at it. I found something that I really enjoyed. Surfing was an escape from home and school.'**

WATER SAFETY

There is an element of risk to surfing. But it is important that you eliminate most of the dangers by using a little bit of common sense and following these water safety rules carefully. After all, you don't want to end your surf career before it's even started! **'People need to have their swimming ability up – if you are going to surf outside of lessons then I think people need to be able to swim at least a couple of hundred metres for their own personal safety.'** This is sound advice from BSA instructor Barrie Hall. Plus the advantage of being a strong swimmer means you'll have good upper body strength, making it easier to paddle and pop.

The golden rule of surfing as Sam Lamiroy explains, is **'Never surf totally by yourself.'** Always go in with a surf coach or a more experienced surfer who can make you aware of potential hazards. If there are just a couple of you in the water, look out for each other. **'An inexperienced surfer out alone is taking their life in their hands,'** explains Sam. **'If you have no one to surf with, find a place where there are lifeguards and just ask them to keep an eye on you. They will know things like where the rips are.'**

'Learn when to say no and know your limits,'

explains Sarah Bentley. You need to be able to read the surf conditions. **'Be aware and watch the waves, see how big they are and look at where other surfers have gone out,'** adds Barrie.

Tides and rips

Twice a day, the tide goes in and out. At high tide, more of the beach will be covered up by the sea, and at low tide, the beach becomes more exposed. As a result, the water is always moving around. A 'rip' is a body of water that is moving across the beach or out to sea through a deeper channel. The rip may move slowly or very fast, creating a 'river' of water. You can usually spot one from the beach as it will generally be a flat area next to where the waves are breaking and the surface will be rippled like a river.

But what should you do if you do get caught in a rip? **'Don't panic!'** says the BSA's Barrie Hall. **'If you do get caught in a rip do not try to battle against it. Paddle across it and out of the rip before coming in.'**

Sarah Bentley also advises, **'A good thing to do**

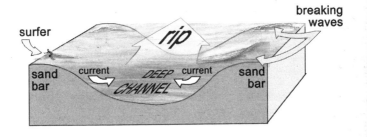

is pick a spot on the beach, something that isn't going to move such as your family or a rock. Line yourself up with it when you get out in the water. You can then check to see if you are drifting. If you are, just paddle back in and walk along to your marker. Then you can go back out and enjoy your session.'

When in the water, remember you are in charge of a 'pointed missile with fins' and so are other learners and surfers. Try to avoid coming into contact with them or swimmers – other people and your surfboard don't mix very well. **'Be aware of your surroundings and be aware of other water users,'** insists Sarah whose unscheduled meeting with another surfer resulted in a few stitches. Wear your leash and keep hold of your board when moving out through the waves. Try not to 'bail your board' or throw it away if a wave comes along – there may be someone behind you and they may not appreciate it!

Other dangers

'Before you go in, check out the area. Look for dangerous things on the beach like rocks and any obstacle that could be a danger like piers and groynes and steer clear of them. Preferably use beaches with lifeguards and ask them for any information,' reminds Barrie Hall.

Other water safety rules may sound obvious but don't go surfing within an hour of eating and if you're getting cold, come in and get warm. Finally, don't go out if it's getting dark. As top European surfer Sam Lamiroy warns, **'Just be sensible. I've seen people get into real trouble by being just a little bit stupid.'**

Warm it up

Warm up properly before you hit the water to avoid any nasty pulls and pains – there's a reason why the pro's do it. **'A warm-up session should be just that, something that warms you up, not the main event. It should take about five minutes and have three main phases to make it effective,'** explains Barrie. First you need to get your body warmed up. **'Running a couple of hundred yards down the beach and back gets your heart going and really begins to loosen you up,'** says top British pro **Gabe Davies**. Next you need to do some gentle stretches. **'Concentrate on your calves, hamstrings and groin with a couple of stretches for the back and some arm circles and loosening movements for the shoulders,'** advises Barrie. **'Finish with simulated movements that you are likely to do in the water, like body twists and pop-ups on the beach.'**

EQUIPMENT NEEDS

Before you get into the water and start ripping it up, you need to know what a surfboard is. There are as many types of board out there as there are people riding them. They all have slightly different characteristics but fall into two main groups – 'longboards' and 'shortboards'. All boards have a 'nose' at the front, 'rails' – the two side edges, and a fin or 'fins' underneath the 'tail' – the rear of the board. The 'deck' is the top where you'll be standing as you tear down the face of the wave. It is also where you apply wax – not to the bottom as some people believe. Your board will always be attached to you by your 'leash', which fixes round the ankle of your back foot. These are the basics – you'll learn more about your equipment later.

Longboards (or Malibus)

As the name suggests, longboards are long – typically over 9ft with one or three fins and a rounded nose. Back in the 1950s these boards were made out of wood and could weigh as much as 25kg. Imagine carrying 25 bags of sugar under one arm! Because they weighed so much they needed to be long and wide to help them float. Although this made them stable, it also made them hard to manoeuvre, which meant that any trick had to be carried out by the surfer on the board as it trimmed along the wave. Popular moves included headstands, spins, walking the board and standing with your toes over the nose (Hanging Ten).

Lightweight materials have revolutionised longboarding, allowing top riders to perform almost every trick a shortboarder can – even aerials. These are the new wave of longboarders, and include riders such as **Bonga Perkins** and **Beau Young**. The 'old skool' style is kept alive by young traditionalists such as 1998 World Longboard Champion **Joel Tudor**.

Due to their size, longboards catch waves very easily and it's not uncommon to see longboarders riding waves even before they have broken. They can also catch small waves, making them good for areas that get less swell. Although this may sound like your ideal board, there are drawbacks – their size makes them impossible to 'duck-dive', hard to control and difficult to carry.

Shortboards

In the late 1960s the average board length dropped from 9 to 7ft over night as surfers literally took a saw to their lightweight foam longboards. By losing the extra 2ft, they gained the ability to ride the whole face of the wave, introducing a whole new style of surfing. From here surfers experimented with every aspect of their board – from length, width, nose rocker and tail design to the number of fins it had on the bottom. By the early Eighties we had arrived at the modern-day 'thruster'. Today, the typical thruster or shortboard is between 6ft and 6ft 6in, with a pointed nose, squashed tail and three fins. Variations on this style of board are pretty much ridden by everyone, from new skool aerialists to big wave riders.

A wide, thick shortboard or mini-mal (with a rounded nose) is a good starting point on your surfing journey. Because they're wide, they're stable but because they're short, they're easier to ride.
(See pp47-51.)

Wetsuits

The poster on your bedroom wall may feature a 'ripper,' charging perfect waves in nothing more than an extremely baggy pair of boardies and a smile. Well, this is where the fantasy ends. The truth is that for probably 80 per cent of your surfing life you will be encased head to toe in rubber, unless you own a holiday home in Fiji. After a surfboard, a good wetsuit is the most important thing you will buy.

As you may have realized, surf speak is based on logic – a shortboard is short, a longboard is long and a wetsuit is designed to keep you wet – not dry as many people believe. Here comes the science bit. Made from a spongy, rubbery material called neoprene, a wetsuit traps a layer of water next to your skin. The water is then warmed by your body heat and acts as a layer of insulation. If your wetsuit leaks like an old tea bag, it will not keep you warm. As Geordie surfer Sam Lamiroy explains, keeping warm is important. **'I think that it really helps to have a good warm wetsuit in a cold area. As long as you are comfortable in the water, no matter what you are doing you'll have fun.'**

One of the commonest mistakes made by a first time surfer is to put the suit on the wrong way round – not a good look. Remember – the zip goes at the back! (See pp 57-60.)

Before you even think about investing in all the equipment, you need to decide if surfing really is for you. Most coastal surf towns have shops where you can hire boards and wetsuits, so a good idea is to try before you buy.

BASIC LESSONS

Your first time in the water will shape your whole future attitude towards surfing. The most important thing is that you should have fun. If you've never surfed before the ideal place to take your first steps, and waves, is at a British Surfing Association (BSA)-registered surf school. You can find these all over the country from the north-east of England to Wales and Cornwall. The list of approved schools is updated annually, so for a full listing check out the BSA's website www.britsurf.co.uk and get ripping!

'BSA instructors have trained officially up to a certain standard and have a beach lifeguard award,' says the UK's National Surfing Centre Head Coach, Barrie Hall. **'There are also safety guidelines the instructors have to work to. Basically you'll know that you are in safe hands.'** As WCT surfer **Russell Winter** explains, **'A friend of ours took us down the beach and gave us some pointers, but surf schools nowadays can teach you much better straight away.'** You will be provided with a wetsuit and foam surfboard – ideal for your first few times as they are safe, stable and light.

Hitting the beach

You've joined up, handed over your cash, and are about to head off for your lesson, but what should you expect to get from your first day at surf school? Well, as Barrie explains, although everyone will progress at a slightly different rate, most first lessons should follow a set formula designed to get you up and riding. Depending on what you book, your lesson should last between 1½ and 3 hours to give you time to pick up the basics. **'After learning about safety we do a brief stretch and warm-up** (see pp15, 29-30) **and go through the equipment and technical terms,'** he says. **'From there we'll explain how to get out into the surf safely – keeping people at waist depth when they're learning. Then we'll concentrate on turning around and**

catching waves in the 'white water' in the 'prone' position, just lying on the boards. This will help with learning to get your balance and understanding where on the board you need to be. We'll cover all of this before you head out, as well as about protection, so when you wipe out and fall off your board you know to cover your head! This part of the lesson is learning all about control, getting your balance and building self confidence.'

When you've mastered about half a dozen controlled rides to the beach on your belly, you're ready to move on to the next phase – paddling and catching a white-water wave yourself.

How to paddle

Lie on your board with your centre of gravity over the centre line, or 'stringer'. Move forwards and backwards until you feel that the board is lying flat and balanced. The nose of the board should not be under the water, or sticking up in the air impersonating the *Titanic*! Lift your head, arching your back so you are looking straight ahead, and paddle one arm at a time as if you are doing the crawl. You need to do this smoothly, keeping as close to the centre line as possible to keep the board stable and to stop it rocking wildly from side to side. Remember the idea is to glide. As with everything in surfing, even this is harder than it sounds. As Cornish Champion Sarah Bentley reveals, **'When I was paddling out, I used to just grit my teeth and think, *You're not going to beat me*. I used to**

**actually talk to the waves and tell them that
I was going to get out there.'**

So you've learnt balance, control, and how to paddle. You're striding back towards the water's edge, and
about 10 metres from the sea you stop, place your
board on the sand, lie on top of it again and start paddling. Hold it! 'Where's the water?' I hear you cry. Well,

the next thing you will learn is how to 'pop' on your board, usually on the beach, in your wetsuit, in the sun. It may look like a scene out of *Point Break* and seem like a crazy thing to do – but it will certainly help you when you try it in the water.

The pop

'Popping up' is when you go from lying to standing on your board. The idea is that you pop to your feet in one fluid movement, as opposed to scrambling to an eventually upright position. **'The key to this is balance and stance on the board, that's why we practise this on the beach,'** explains top BSA Coach, Barrie Hall.

To pop up, as with paddling, lie on your stomach in the middle of your board, with your feet over the fins. Place the palms of your hands on your board under your shoulders. Arch your back, keeping your head up, and lever your body as if you are going to do a press-up. At the same time bring your front foot forward and under your stomach. Push down with your front foot, making your body rise until you are standing in a crouched position with your bum in, shoulders square to the board, facing forward. Your back foot should be over the fins, placed flat and horizontal to the board while your front foot should be in the middle of the board, again placed flat at a 45° angle to your back foot. It's hard at first but the idea is that you do this all in one fluid motion! If you try to stand up straight, you'll just fall off again so you need to keep your centre of gravity low and your knees bent. Now you know why it's a good idea to practise on the land first!

Best foot forward

You'll probably have heard your favourite surfers talking about being goofy or regular. This has nothing to do with trips to the dentist, it's all to do with which foot you put at the front of the board and which foot you put your leash on. If you ride with your left foot forward you are 'regular' or 'natural', with your right foot you are 'goofy'.

Which foot forward you ride with has no effect on your surfing ability – 2001 World Champion CJ Hobgood is a goofy footer where as four-times women's World Champion Lisa Andersen rides regular. As a general rule, if you skateboard or snowboard, you will already know which foot forward feels comfortable to ride on. If not, stand with your feet next to each other and get someone you know to push you from behind. If you step forward with your left foot, then this foot naturally wants to go first and you are regular. If your right foot goes forward first then you are goofy. This is only a general rule so try it out and make sure it feels comfortable to you. If not, try swapping it around.

Up and riding

'Once you master your pop on land, the last part of the lesson is spent in the water, getting people up and running and hopefully getting people standing up, which is the fun part,' says Barrie. If you look at a beach you will usually see waves breaking and forming white-water rollers. These will probably be breaking in one place more than in another. This shows there is a sandbank and the water is shallower, causing the waves to break. At this stage, the white water close to the beach is exactly where you want to head for. Do not get out of your depth. Everyone starts in the small surf, as Quiksilver's surf team manager **Peyo Lizarazu** recalls. **'When I started surfing, I learnt on the flattest beach on the whole coast, with the weakest waves.'** By the age of 13, Peyo was the Junior European Surfing Champion.

Catching and riding a white-water wave

Lie on your board in the paddle position, facing the beach. Look over your shoulder and as you see the white-water approaching, begin paddling towards the beach making sure that your path is free from other surfers and water users. The idea is that you are travelling at the same speed as the wave by the time it reaches you. If not it will simply break over you, usually catapulting you off your board. As the white-water picks you up, you will feel yourself accelerate forward. This is the point where you can stop paddling and try to pop to your feet. This is MUCH harder than it is on the beach as your board seems to take on a mind of its own and tries to bounce you off at every opportunity. As soon as you're upright, stay low and balanced. Don't worry about falling off – a fact of surfing life is that everyone does. One thing to remember is not to jump off head first – the water you're learning in is pretty shallow and a neck brace may cramp your style.

If you want to take up surfing, the BSA recommends that you have at least three lessons, but between five and ten lessons will give you a firm base to improve on and get you progressing out of the white water and on to the green. But as Gabe Davies says, **'It takes a long time to learn how to paddle out, a long time to learn how to read the waves, and a long time to learn how to stand up and duck-dive. I'm still learning now – you're learning all the time.'** So stick with it; if it was easy it wouldn't be half the challenge or half as much fun!

Getting on to the open face

Once you've got the white water wired, it's time to head out for some unbroken wave action. In theory it is the same as catching a white-water wave, but in practice it's a whole new skill.

For this you need to understand a bit about waves and how they work. As a wave approaches the beach, the water gets gradually shallower, which causes the waves to steepen and eventually break. If you have sat and watched surfers you will have seen that for short-boarders, the best place to be when catching a wave is next to the 'curl' – near the part of the wave that is actually breaking. This is because it is the steepest part of the wave and will help to propel you on to the open face. (As we have mentioned before, longboarders can catch waves before they have even broken and so being next to the curl is less critical for them.)

As with catching white water, you need to start paddling before the wave arrives but this time you also need to be in the critical position on the wave – the part where it is steep and about to break. This is where judgement and timing come in. If you start paddling too soon, you will be too far ahead of the wave and either be pitched over with the 'lip' or only catch the white water. If you start paddling too late, the wave will not be steep enough and you will simply be left behind. It may be frustrating at first but the secret to perfecting your timing

is to just keep trying. **'Don't be put off the first time you try it and think, *This is hard, I'll never be able to do it,'** explains Sarah Bentley. **'Be patient and it will come.'**

Having watched from the beach, paddle out to the line-up, sitting just behind where the biggest waves or 'set waves' are breaking. Sit and watch as a few sets come through so you can judge where and when the waves break – the bigger waves will break further out and the smaller ones closer in. You can also pick up tips just by watching other surfers in the water. The wave will be breaking either to the left or right so a good tip is to slightly angle your board in that direction when you paddle for it. As with riding white water, if you have timed it right, you will feel the wave pick up your board and begin to carry you forward, at which stage you need to pop to your feet. As your board is angled, it will be moving on to the open face. If not, lean gently into the wave.

Control

Learning control of your stick will be your ticket to ride. You'll soon be ripping it up or at the very least be able to get out of the way of other surfers. When you're going along the open face, experiment with subtly shifting your weight over either 'rail' or board edge. You will find yourself climbing and dropping down the face of the wave, or 'trimming'. This can help you to gain speed on smaller waves and steer around obstacles in your path. If you exaggerate your lean, you will either straighten out and head towards the beach or 'pull out', coming off the back of the wave – useful if you see that the wave is going to 'close out' or if someone's in your way.

TECHNIQUE: Practice makes perfect

'Mum, where's the ironing board?'

One of the best tips I was given when learning was to practice surfing in my bedroom. Obviously you can't paddle or turn, but you can practise your 'pop'. A good pop is the most important part of surfing, and the more you pop, the easier it is. It also helps to build up those important muscles. **'Make a surfboard shape out of tape on your bedroom floor,'** explains Sarah Bentley. **'Just keep popping up on that shape and getting your feet in the right place.'**

And now, the best piece of homework you'll ever be given – watching surf videos. Watch how the pros pop up, their stance, where they are looking and how they turn the board. Or see if you can tempt your dad on to the beach with a camcorder to record your moves. You can watch your session with a critical eye and see what you're doing right and, more importantly, where you're going wrong.

But there's no substitute for the real thing. **'The best way to practise surfing is to go surfing,'** says former World Champion **Barton Lynch**.

Exercise to stay surf fit

With a lesson lasting up to three hours and a surf session lasting as long as the waves keep pumping, you're going to need stamina! **'To keep yourself active for that long you do need a reasonable amount of fitness,'** says Barrie Hall. He and a lot of other top surfers recommend swimming in-between sessions, particularly front crawl. It is a good aerobic sport which means that it pushes your heart and lungs to work that bit harder. Using a similar movement to paddling, it helps you to develop upper body muscles important for surfing. Not only do you use these for paddling they are also crucial to developing a good pop. It will also help to develop water confidence. Aside from swimming, both the BSA and top European rider Gabe Davies recommend plenty of stretches on a daily basis and advise giving yoga a go.

To help work on your balance when you are away from the surf, Barrie Hall recommends trying other board sports such as skateboarding and snowboarding. Skateboarding is pretty accessible to most people living in an urban area – all you need is a quiet patch of flat road or pavement and a basic board which you can pick up from a skate shop or even a catalogue shop from around £30 upwards.

TRICKS AND MANOEUVRES

Now you're out on the open face it's time to show off your surf tricks.

Bottom turn

The smoothest surfer on the planet is Tom Curren. **'To me the bottom turn is the most important manoeuvre a surfer performs. You have to be smooth to carry your speed out on to the open face, setting yourself up for your first manoeuvre,'** says the three-times World Champion. When you reach the bottom of the wave after taking the drop, you will have a lot of momentum. Turn too hard and the speed will be lost, not enough and you will simply not get on to the open face. When dropping down

the face, you need to keep your knees bent slightly, and you should be looking at where on the face you want to go.

The key to a good turn is how you shift your body weight. When you reach the bottom of the wave and are about to start your turn, you need to make sure that your weight is very slightly over the back foot and fins. By pushing down on your toes, you will cause the rail and the fins to bite into the face of the wave, which will turn the board on to your 'front side' so you will be facing the wave. Or by pressing down slightly on your heel side, you will cause your fins and rail to turn the board on to your 'back hand' (with your back to the wave) and out on to the open face. You need to keep your knees bent and bottom in and focus on where you are going.

When you start, you will be trying to turn in a smooth arc out on to the open face and along the wave. As you progress, you can aim to make your bottom turn a bit tighter so that you will carve up the face to set up a manoeuvre such as a 'slash' off the top or an 'aerial'.

Cutback

Modern surfing with its speed and powerful turns is possible because surfers ride in the 'pocket' – the steepest part of the wave. The cutback is designed to get the surfer back into the pocket, where the speed is greatest, from out on the open face, where momentum can be lost. A cutback is in effect turning back on yourself to generate more speed.

Duck dive

There's only one thing standing in between you and getting out the back – that wave coming right for you. In order to get out into the line-up you will have to learn how to 'duck-dive' you and your board under the waves. This is the most underestimated part of a surfer's skills. Paddle towards the breaking wave, and as it approaches, sink the front of your board by raising your body as if you are doing a push-up. At the same time you need to push the nose of your board down under the wave. Bend your arms, keeping a firm hold of your board, take a breath and as the wave meets you, duck your head and whole body under it. Place your knee in the middle of the board and raise your other leg in the air.

In theory your board should sink and you should pass under the advancing wave and appear on the other side. In practice you may find your board flying out behind you or between your legs. **'I think the hardest thing to learn for me was getting out through the waves – learning to duck-dive,'** says top European surfer **Kepa Acero**.

Try practising in small waves when there are no surfers

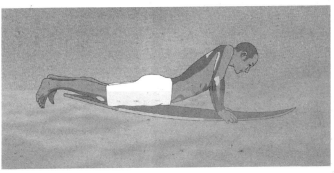

behind you. **'Duck-diving was super-hard,'** says former British Champion Gabe Davies. **'That was when I was little and the board was really big, so at the time it felt like you needed brute strength but in reality a lot of it is down to technique.'** Once you have mastered the duck dive you will be ready to take your place in the line-up.

ADVANCED TRICKS

Now you've mastered the basics, it's time to grab some airtime or check out the 'green room'…

Tail slide

A tail slide is a variation on an 'off the lip'. As you turn high on the face of the wave, un-weight the tail and punch it round with your back foot so that it breaks free of the water at the top of the wave. If you do this right it should throw a plume of spray and look insane from the line-up.

Floaters

Now you've mastered turning up the face of the wave it's time to have a go at a floater. The floater originated at beach breaks where the wave would have a 'close-out section' – a small area breaking ahead of the curl. In order to get around this section the surfer would ride up the face, over the close-out section and back on to the wave. Floaters are now a part of every surfer's arsenal.

To pull off a floater, generate speed down the line, turn

up the face and launch on to the top of the breaking wave. Your speed should help you to slide along the top of the curl. As you start to lose speed turn towards the shore and the breaking wave should bring you back down off the lip and on to the face again. This is a great finale to any ride.

New-skool moves include an aerial-to-floater combination or a floater with a 180 or 360 spinning re-entry.

360

A 360 is where a surfer rotates their board in a full turn. This classic trick brought from the skate parks and into the water is a favourite move in small surf on the new light boards with smaller fins. By shifting your weight forward, your fins will be lifted out of the water at the back of the board. Turn your upper body first in the direction you want

to rotate, followed by your lower body and push the tail of the board round. The fins are no longer biting into the water, so what you are performing is an exaggerated tail slide. Keep your centre of balance low and over the board. If you do this right you should find yourself riding backwards. You have just done a 180. With your weight still towards the front of the board, twist your upper-body again and pull the tail round so that you are facing the right way again. The movement should be fluid and smooth. While you are spinning, keep your weight in the middle of the board as it is easy to catch a rail and be thrown off.

Aerials

Still the ultimate new-skool move, the aerial has been around since the Eighties. Speed needs to be generated down the line, and the lip of the wave needs to be used like a ramp. Once up to speed, launch yourself up the face of the wave. Surfers like **Nathan Fletcher** and Cory Lopez use skate techniques to get extra height into their aerials. As they hit the top of the lip they drag their front foot up the board towards the nose, scraping the deck with the outside of their foot, causing the tail to rise (like a lever) so that the board will become level in the air. This is an 'ollie'. It gives aerials more air, and makes them easier to land – and landing your aerial is everything!

Barrels

The tube ride is the ultimate surfing move. First you need a hollow wave. Watch the wave to see the best take-off point, and watch how it peels. If you are riding frontside, angle your take-off away from the peak slightly, drop in and turn on to the face, keeping a low line – if you travel too high you may get pitched. Barrelling waves are by nature steep so if you are moving too fast you can regulate your speed by trailing a hand in the face of the wave. If you are in the right position you should see the lip of the wave curling over your head. Stay low and compact and enjoy the ride. A barrel may only last a second or two but it will feel like you were in there for hours.

Backside tube rides are harder to master. Crouch low and grab the rail of your board with your outside hand. This is called 'pig dogging' and gives extra stability. Pull your back leg in and to cut speed, trail your inside hand in the face of the wave. Stay low and hang on.

Comfort zones

Surfing is all about progression. When you start learning, the white water is your comfort zone – you know how it works and what to expect. The line-up is the unknown.

As you progress into the line-up of your local beach, 3 or 4ft surf may be where you feel comfortable, whereas your confidence falters in bigger waves or at the thought of surfing the local reef break. Some people progress quickly on to bigger waves or better breaks, other take a bit more time. Some never move out of their original comfort zones.

It's important to push your surfing at a good steady

pace. Surfing with friends will help. **'It's very difficult to push yourself when you're alone,'** says Sam Lamiroy. **'If you have a choice of surfing where there are a few more surfers, do it, because everyone is competitive. You see your friends doing a manoeuvre and you want to try it too.'**

But remember, never surf in waves that are beyond you. It's about a steady progression, not massive leaps. If you are comfortable in 3ft surf, don't be tempted to go out in 6-8ft. Be patient.

Surfing bigger waves

Everyone is scared of bigger waves to start with, even six-times World Champion Kelly Slater. **'I was scared of big waves. People used to make fun of me!** Brock Little **made fun of me all my years grow-ing up in Hawaii.'** Kelly has proved time and time again that you can overcome a fear of large surf. After surfing in a number of big waves events, 2002 saw him win the Quiksilver Eddie Aikau big-wave competition in 25-30ft waves.

Even top Portuguese world tour surfer **Tiago Pires** admits **'I still get scared. Not the kind of scared that freezes you, the kind of scared that amps you, makes you aware. In Hawaii I surf big waves and when I'm in the barrel I'm fright-ened but when I come out it's like "Yes!"'**

To surf big waves you need good skills and a different type of surfboard called a 'gun'. A big-wave board can be anything between 7ft for a semi-gun to 8 to 9ft for a gun. Unlike a longboard they have a narrow pin-tail, pointed nose and three fins – like a stretched thruster. Guns have to be long to help the surfer catch bigger waves. These waves tend to be moving faster than smaller waves and the bigger board allows the surfer to get up and riding sooner, essential for big-wave riding. One of the worst things that can happen to a big-wave surfer is to be caught at the top of the wave, without the speed to make the drop down before the wave breaks. This can result in the surfer being pitched over with the wave and plunged deep underwater.

As surfers have pushed the boundaries of big-wave riding, it has reached a point where they are tackling waves too big to be paddled into. Waves above a certain size travel faster than a surfer can paddle and become too dangerous to surf. This led to the invention of 'tow-in surfing.' (Check out Laird Hamilton, on pp127-8.)

SURFING COMMANDMENTS

Over the years surfing has developed a set of rules to keep the line-up safe and to prevent it descending into total anarchy. These 'rules' are there to protect everyone and help to make sure your session is a good one. Remember, it's supposed to be fun!

Drop-ins – DO NOT drop into a wave that another surfer, who is nearer to the curl, is already riding on. This is the number one rule in surfing.

'Be aware of other water users,' says Cornwall's Sarah Bentley.

When the water is busy and there are few waves, it is tempting to try and paddle for every one. Stop! You need to remember that the waves are for everyone and you will have to wait your turn. Use your eyes and ears to check if someone is already up and riding. If they are, let them enjoy it – it'll be your turn soon. Dropping in on someone isn't just annoying – it can be dangerous too.

Accidents can happen as surfers collide, boards fly in the air and leashes get tangled up.

Priority – The surfer nearest to the curl ALWAYS has priority to go.

'Next to the curl is the best place to take off but not the easiest so you find that the best surfers or the locals who know the

The surfer on the right has priority

break will usually be in this position, sitting on the peak,' explains travelling pro, Sam Lamiroy. If you're learning you'll have to hope you can pick up some smaller waves on the 'inside' as you work your way up the pecking order.

Paddling out – DO NOT get in the way of a surfer who's up and riding while you are paddling out.

At point and reef breaks use the channels to get out and just keep your eyes open at beach breaks.

Snaking – DO NOT try to paddle round a surfer who is already paddling for a wave in an attempt to get closer to the peak and steal their wave.

Localism – DO NOT intimidate surfers who come to your break.

'Travel is such a major part of surfing. You should treat visiting surfers as you would like to be treated at their break,' says travelling free-surfer, Gabe Davies. Don't become a playground bully, remember what goes around comes around!

Wave hogs – DO NOT steal all the waves.

Nobody likes a wave hog so share the waves and create a good vibe in the water.

Bailing – DO NOT bail your board and let it fly out behind you.

When a wave is heading your way and you haven't mastered duck-diving, take a look around before you bail your board. If there are surfers behind you just keep hold of it. You won't make friends by introducing them to the sharp end of your board!

4
Equipment

BOARDS

'I started surfing when I was eleven. My first board was a very old, dodgy, 5ft 8in, 1970's board which I shared with my brother. It had only one fin, when it was supposed to have two, which made it completely off balance. We fixed it up and we didn't know any better so we thought this surfboard was the best surfboard in the world. We went in the water, loved it, and have been in the water ever since.' Gabe Davies.

Your first board

So you've tried surfing, you liked it and now it's time for your first real relationship. It is a relationship you will never forget – the relationship between a surfer and their first board. Four-times World Champ Lisa Andersen went for the colour. **'My first board was pink, I can see it now. I wish I still had it.'**

'When I was at home in Reunion I was still body-boarding and my father came to the beach one day with a brand new surfboard for me and he called me over and said "This is for you!" and I couldn't believe it!' recalls pro surfer **Fredrick Robin**. German surfer **Marlon Lipke** was another who started out on a body board. **'I**

started when I was about five. Then I got this polystyrene board which I stood up on in the white water for maybe three years. When I got my first real surfboard for Christmas, I was stoked.' As Tiago Pires of Portugal says, the idea is to just get out in the water. **'I started boogie boarding. I didn't care – I just wanted to get in the water and have some fun. My boogie board wasn't even a good one. I went with my friends and older brother. He started surfing before me and he just pushed me into surfing when I was about eleven.'**

For your first equipment purchases there's no need to go out and buy an expensive performance board, which can be upwards of £300, plus a brand new wetsuit. Save your money for when you have progressed and will need to invest in better equipment. If there's one mistake that beginners make before even getting in the water, it is to buy the wrong board to learn on. **'A good shaper or shop owner will advise a beginner to buy a board that is stable and easy to paddle,'** explains ODD board-shaper Paul Gill. **'Don't go to a shaper determined to have the latest pro-model. They'll be thin and narrow and not stable enough to learn on.'**

He's riding a fish?

So now you've had some lessons on a foamy and you are looking for your first 'real' surfboard. There are as many types of surfboard out there as there are surfers in the sea. It will all seem a bit confusing at first but when you cut through the jargon, it's all pretty simple. The basic model types are as follows:

A **fish** is a short, wide, three-finned board, usually with a 'swallow tail' (see p. 55) and pointed nose. Designed for small waves, the extra width and volume give them more speed and drive in weaker waves.

A **shortboard** is the board most surfers ride. It can be any combination of length (up to 7ft) and width to suit the conditions and the surfer. Wider, thicker boards are good for small surf; narrow pin-tail boards are good for bigger surf.

A **mini-mal** takes the good points of a short board and mixes them with the good points of a long board. It has a rounded nose, is wide and stable, easy to paddle and catches lots of waves but is not as manoeuvrable as a shortboard and is very hard to duck dive.

A **gun** is a classic big-wave board. It is usually between 8 and 9ft long, has three fins, a pointed nose and a pin tail. The length of the board allows the surfer to paddle into the big waves (15-20ft) more easily. A mini-gun is usually between 7 and 8ft for large (8-15ft) waves.

A **longboard** is a classic, which is usually 9ft or longer, has a rounded nose, is very wide and has either one or three fins.

A **quiver** is the term used for a range of boards designed for various conditions, for example a professional surfer may take a quiver of ten boards to Hawaii for the season.

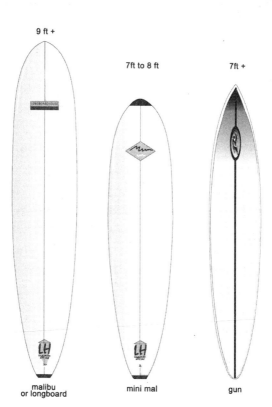

9 ft +

malibu
or longboard

7ft to 8 ft

mini mal

7ft +

gun

thruster

fish

50

What to avoid in a second-hand board

When looking for your first board there is one golden rule: Don't be blinded by a nice spray job or sponsors' stickers! There are only three things to remember when buying your first board, it should be cheap, it should be functional and you've got to love it. **'I had quite a love-hate relationship which I think you normally do with your first board,'** confesses Sarah Bentley, **'where one day you think it's the greatest thing you've got and the next day you want to chuck it in the bin.'**

A modern surfboard has a polyurethane foam core which is wrapped in fibreglass cloth and coated in a layer of clear varnish, or 'glassed'. The foam gives the board its lightness and buoyancy and the fibreglass and varnish give it strength. Before you part with your hard-earned cash, make sure you give it a thorough examination first. Watch out for the following:

Cracks – Unfortunately surfboards are quite fragile and if the glass is punctured or cracked, water can seep into the foam core and cause discolouration and the foam to rot. You can see if there is rot as that area will be soft. Small cracks can be fixed if the foam has not been damaged. 'Solarez' is a must for any surfer's bag. This tube of gel fills holes and hardens to form a tough seal, allowing dings or punctures to be fixed in minutes.

Dings – Older boards may be covered with little dents that have not actually punctured the surface and are caused by knees or feet. A few on the deck are OK but there should not be too many on the underside of the board.

Creases – These occur when a board has been hit by the lip of a wave with enough power to bend it. The telltale signs are a crease line or crack in the glass running around the bottom or top of the board. These boards should be avoided.

Broken boards – These are often repaired and put up for sale. Repairs can be seen as patches around the middle or areas where the board has been painted white to try to mask the repair job. While some repaired boards are structurally strong, they are also best avoided.

Fins – These should be checked to make sure they are not cracked around the base or loose.

Second-hand boards may cost from £10 to £150. Surf shops are the most obvious place to look but if you are on a limited budget, a top tip is to ask around at the beach. A lot of surfers still have the board they learnt on and may be willing to sell it on. Check newspaper classified adverts or Exchange and Mart. If you live near the coast then garage sales are also worth going to. There are a lot of 'lost' surfboards out there just looking for a home but whoever you buy from, make sure you actually see the board before you agree to a sale. When you want to upgrade, ask around as surf shops often do trade-ins.

The shaper

So when should you start to think about moving up to a custom board? **'I'd say you need to start concentrating on your equipment when you're getting to the stage of taking off on waves and bottom turning and turning on**

the face,' explains Sam Lamiroy. **'That's the point when you have enough of an under-standing of surfing to go to the shaper you want to make your board and talk to them. Unless you are some kind of a design genius, you will not have enough experience or insight to know what will work.'** But that's where the experience of the guy who makes your board, 'the shaper', comes in.

'One of the critical things of going and talking to your shaper is that you need to be brutally honest with yourself and him,' explains one of the UK's leading shapers and owner of Beach Beat surfboards, Chops Lascelles. **'It's a bit like going to the doctor. Be truthful about your ability, not what you think it is or would like it to be, and also about your height and weight. All these factors deter-mine what type of board you'll need.'**

So what are the most important design aspects when choosing a first surfboard? **'I think it's a com-bination of length, width and thickness,'** says four-times World Champion and leading shaper Mark Richards. **'I think they are the three factors that make a surfboard work. You can have all kinds of concaves in a board, edges and all the groovy stuff, but if the length, width and thickness isn't right for the rider on top of it, no amount of concave or groovy stuff will make the board go.'**

Stability is determined mainly by its width, and also by a board's thickness and length. A wide board is a good starting point. But what does a shaper mean when he talks about rockers and rails? Before you buy, you need to get up close and personal with a board and be familiar with the role of each board part.

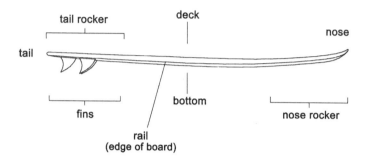

'A nose "rocker" is the curve at the front of the board, a bit like the bow of a ship. It stops the nose digging into the water and "pearling", but if you make it too harsh, the board will push water in front of it and slow down,' says Paul Gill.

A modern shortboard is designed for the new style of surfing. As Chops explains, 'A modern young surfer stays on the back end of a surfboard, like a skater. They stand on the tail of the skateboard to lift the front up and turn – instead of wheels as a pivot at the back, it's fins.' A tail rocker helps this style of surfing, like the curve on the tail of a skateboard.

The rails are the edges of the board and are described as 'hard' if they are angular or 'soft' when they are more rounded. 'When you do a turn or slide, the edge bites into the wave – the

harder the edge the better the bite,' says Chops.

There are different tails for different surf conditions. A narrow or pin tail makes a board more stable in steeper or larger waves because with a small surface area it allows the water to flow easily around it and stops the board being pulled up the face. A wide or squash tail is better for smaller waves as with a larger surface area, it gives the board more forward drive, but this also makes it harder to turn. A swallow tail is like a squash tail with a 'V' cut out of it, combining good thrust with manoeuvrability.

If you want to know more about the ins and outs of board design check out:
www.beachbeatsurfboards.co.uk

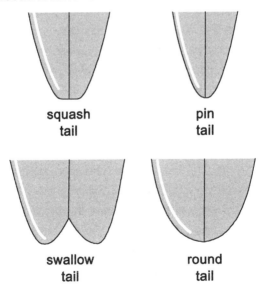

squash
tail

pin
tail

swallow
tail

round
tail

Off with his fins!

Removable fins systems, like FCS, have revolutionised

surfing. Undo the little screws that hold them in place and you can experiment with different size fins for different conditions. It also means that your boards are easier to pack – although it is one more thing to remember!

Board price guide

Having a surfboard custom made by a shaper is no more expensive than buying one off the shelf in a shop. Although it may sound like a lot of money, a shaper and glasser will have spent many hours making you a personal, custom board by hand, which has been designed for your skill level and the type of waves you want to surf. **'It basically takes a week to make a surfboard,'** says Chops. **'It takes a day to shape it and spray it, a good day to glass it – that is the most important part, another to sand it smooth and put all the fin fittings in, a day to finish it and a day to polish it. A lot of people are amazed by how much work goes into just one board.'**

A shaper will probably charge between £350 and £400 for a new custom thruster. Prices vary depending on things like the finish, tail design (swallow tails may cost more), spray jobs and the type of fins you order (FCS or glassed). Longboards can cost between £400 and £500.

Board customisation

Stickers are a great way of turning your trusty stick into a customised flyer like the pro's ride. A few quid wisely invested at your local surf shop, or a couple of letters sent to your favourite surf brand can transform even the dullest board.

Waterproof, wide tip felt markers are available in a range of colours and will transform a standard white board into a work of art. Many of the top pro's customise their boards in this way. Favourite drawings include cartoon characters and multi-coloured patterns or flags. If art isn't your thing, why not ask one of your arty friends or brother or sister. Check out the latest *Surfer* or *Surfing* magazines for ideas.

Remember you should love your first board. **'People sometimes say their first board was their worst board,'** says Sam Lamiroy, **'but I think that's wrong. People shouldn't say that because that's the board that got them surfing. It should be the best one.'**

How to look after your stick

So now you have the board, you have to look after it. Here are some tips to keep your board in tip-top shape.

➤ Don't put it down on the rocks – it will get dinged. Surfboards are fragile.

➤ Don't leave it in the sun – it'll go brown like your toast! If it gets too hot the wax will melt everywhere. Keep your board in the shade and always apply a light fresh coat of wax before going in the water.

➤ Get a bag. If a bag's a bit expensive, get a sock or make one. A home-made sock can be cooler than a shop-bought one.

➤ Repair those dings. If the glass gets punctured

then water will get in. Invest in a tube of Solarez and fix dings as soon as possible.

➤ Watch your fins! Older boards that have been around a bit sometimes have sharp edges on their fins. These can be dangerous and can cut you or your wetsuit. Blunt any sharp edges with sandpaper.

➤ Check your leash for nicks. Sharp fins can sometimes leave little cuts in your leash. If they do you will need to replace it. The last thing you want is a snapped leash and your board being swept away on to nearby rocks.

WETSUITS

Wetsuits are made of a spongy, rubbery material called neoprene. Wetsuits work by trapping a layer of water next to the skin, which is warmed by body heat. The combination of the neoprene and warm water keeps the body insulated from the colder sea.

Your wetsuit will be a very important buy and a bad wetsuit will mean you get cold quickly and surf less. Find the right suit for you and enjoy hours out in the water.

Wetsuits come in a range of thicknesses. A 4/3 suit will have 4mm neoprene around the body and 3mm neoprene around the legs and arms. This is a good thickness for Cornwall in the autumn, winter and spring. In the summer a 3/2 will be OK. On the East Coast you will need a thicker 5/4/3 suit as the water temperatures here can drop to 5 or 6 degrees in the winter. In the summer a 4/3 will do here.

The style of suit on offer falls into the following groups. A 'shortie' is a wetsuit with short sleeves and short legs.

These are usually thin summer suits for warmer water. A 'spring suit' usually has short sleeves and long legs and is designed for warm to cool water – like Cornwall in the summer. A 'steamer' has long legs and sleeves and is designed for cool to cold water. Some 5/4/3 suits have 'hoods' to keep your head warm. It's also worth investing in a good pair of 'gloves' and 'booties' for when the colder weather kicks in.

There are also different cuts of wetsuits with most companies now producing suits specifically for girls. You'll also be faced by shoulder zips, chest zips or even zipperless suits as well as insulators in the neoprene, like titanium or copper. Upgraded elastic and stretchy suits are coming out all the time.

Buying a second-hand suit

Grommets usually have a rapidly expanding body but a limited budget. It will probably be unfeasibly expensive to buy a brand new wetsuit every six months, so the best bet is a good quality second-hand suit. Most surf shops will do a trade-in when it's time to up size. **'We've got boards and wetsuits here that we just keep swapping over,'** says Chops. **'So many kids have started off on the same board and same wetsuit from our shop. You may lose 30 or 40 quid on a board or 20 quid on a wetsuit but it's affordable.'** Always try the suits on and make sure they are not too baggy, or they will leak, or if they're too tight you'll have no room to grow or move!

What to look for: The most important thing to look for in a wetsuit is not this season's hottest colours, but that it is designed for surfing – not diving. Make sure the suit you buy is warm enough for where you are going to surf. Also, if you are in a cold water area, make sure the suit has blind-stitched or glued and taped seams, otherwise water can seep in. Make sure there are no tears or holes and always check that the zip works. But the most important thing to look for in a wetsuit is the correct fit.

Buying a new suit: There is nothing quite like the feeling of pulling on a new wetsuit. So if you're going to invest your hard-earned cash in a new suit, make sure it's the right one. Get a really good fit, get the right thickness, check you have the right seams and check you can get out of it by yourself! Good British brands to look out for include Snugg, Second Skin, Gul and Alder. Major surf brands include Quiksilver, Roxy, Rip Curl, O'Neill and Billabong

How to look after your suit: There is only one golden rule when it comes to looking after your wetsuit: always rinse it out with fresh water or it will begin to smell and the seams will rot. Also, if you get any holes or tears, repair them quickly (with rubber glue available from surf shops) as small tears will grow and become harder to mend.

ACCESSORIES

Leashes – Up until the 1970s surfers used to ride without leashes. Falling off could mean a long swim, sometimes all the way to the beach. It's hard to believe that when leashes were invented there was hostility towards them – they were referred to as 'kook-cords' by some.

A good leash is now essential and they come in different lengths, longer ones for longboarders and big wave riders, normal leashes (designed for thrusters) and smaller, lightweight leashes for summer surf. And don't forget, the leash goes around the ankle of your trailing foot.

Helmets – Many top surfers use helmets when surfing reef breaks or in crowded areas. You are just as likely to get hit by a flying board as you are to get bounced on to a rocky reef. Remember you only have one head – use it. Check out Gath and Gecko helmets in your surf shop.

Noseguards – A noseguard or nosecone will set you back between £10 and £15 but is an essential investment. The rubbery material stops the pointed end of your board becoming a dangerous missile and can save you from serious injury.

Wax – Wax is rubbed on the upper surface of the board to make it grippy, allowing you not only to lie on your board, but also to pop to your feet. The waxy deck of a surfboard allows enough traction to turn the board and even pop aerials without slipping off. In the chilly north-east waters, a cold water wax is needed whereas in Cornwall a cool water wax is probably better.

A 'deck grip' is a small square of a spongy, matt-like material produced by companies like Gorilla Grip, which is glued to the deck of the board where the rear foot goes. Over the years many inventions have been put forward to replace wax but even after all these years it is still the surfers' number one choice!

5
Surf travel

For 90 per cent of grommets, getting to the beach can be harder than learning to surf. Unless you are one of the lucky few who live within walking/cycling distance of the sea, you will need a lift. And this is where your first real sponsorship deal comes in. Sympathetic parents, older brothers/sisters, or friends will be your first surf sponsors. OK, so they won't require sticker placement on your board, but they may demand car-washing or baby-sitting duties. As WCT surfer Russell Winter says, **'Having a caring father or mother is the most important sponsorship. My mum and dad helped me out a lot!'** So if you live inland, do not despair.

But there is more to surf travel than merely getting to your local beach. Surfing and travel are as closely linked as Siamese twins. The classic surf trip is as important a part of surf culture as the actual wave-riding itself. Whether it's checking out all your local breaks with your mates or your first surf holiday to a foreign beach, surf travel is a bug that will be with you as long as you enjoy riding waves.

TRAVEL IN THE UK

So now you know the basics of how to surf, you may want to practise what you've learnt somewhere new. Here's a lowdown of some of the UK's top beaches. This rough guide should get you started but remember there are hundreds of spots around the UK and chatting to locals will give you a good idea of the other breaks to check out.

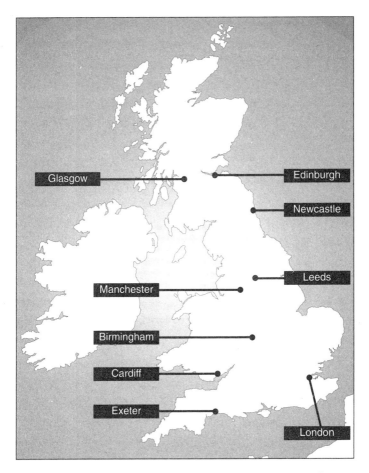

'The best thing you can invest in is a good map that shows all the beaches,' says British surfer Sarah Bentley. **'You can use it to help work out which beach will be good in a certain wind direction or on a certain swell so you don't have too many wasted trips.'**

Learning to surf new places, and learning to 'read' new breaks will really push your surfing. But remember that water safety has to come first – before surfing a new spot make sure you check it out properly. (*See Water Safety,pp12-13*)

Cornwall

When most people think of surfing in the UK, the first place that comes to mind is Cornwall. Newquay is flooded with international surfers every summer when the annual Boardmasters hits town. As well as being easily accessible, with loads of places to stay and a lively social surf scene, Cornwall gets a good amount of swell. If you add this to the fact that it has the warmest water in the UK – up to 5° warmer than the chilly north east – it is no surprise that the line-up can get crowded, especially in the summer.

Here are a few Cornish hot spots to get you started:

1 Gwithian – a long sandy beach north of St Ives that is good for surfers of all abilities. It is offshore in a south-easterly wind.

2 Porthtowan – sandy beach south of St Agnes with good parking. Lifeguards in summer and a seasonal surf shop with board hire.

3 Perranporth – a good spot for beginners as it has a long and gradually sloping beach. Parking next to the beach means good access and there are lifeguards in the summer. Good equipment hire.

4 Newquay – known as the surf capital of the UK, the number of surf shops in Newquay is in double figures and rising all the time. A good place to visit out of season or, after a quiet summer, to pick up a few bargains. It is a popular spot for beginners/young surfers in the summer and the water can be very busy. A good place for beginners to head for would be the Town Beaches or Watergate. Fistral beach is the home of the National Surfing Centre where you can get lessons from BSA instructors. Intermediates could head for Watergate or Fistral where the surf can be excellent.

5 Widemouth Bay – sandy beach to the south of Bude, Widemouth is a popular beach with banks along its length.

6 Bude – a number of beaches on a long stretch of sand that runs north from Bude; it has something for all abilities.

7 Porthleven – best left to the experts, this gnarly wave is the south's most respected reef and definitely somewhere to just watch and learn.

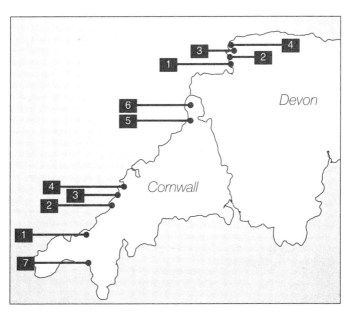

North Devon

North Devon has a large local surf population and booming surf industry. It also regularly plays host to a number of contests including the British and English Surfing

Championships. When westerly swells combine with easterly winds it becomes a true surfer's paradise.

1 Saunton – huge, gently sloping beach, the waves here are less powerful and therefore a good place to learn.

2 Croyde – top quality beach break for the intermediate to experienced, that can get crowded.

3 Putsburough – a more sheltered spot around the corner from Croyde which is good when Croyde is big and blown out.

4 Woolacombe – a less crowded alternative worth considering.

South Coast

Although the south coast does not have great quality waves and is vulnerable to the wind, it still has a committed surf community who will be out there at every opportunity. So if you live nearby or are visiting your Aunty Vi, go and join them! Places to check out include:

Bournemouth and **Brighton Pier**, **Southbourne**, **Eastbourne** and the **Isle of Wight** – which picks up more swell and even hosts its own annual surf competition.

East Coast

Although the water is not as warm and welcoming as Cornwall, the east coast has some first class breaks and first class surfers. Autumn and spring offer the best surf conditions for this region but remember to wrap up warmly – hoods, gloves and boots are often essential. The Northumberland coastline, with abandoned castles overlooking its beaches, remains the UK's least

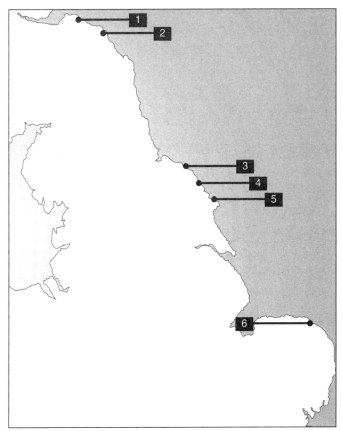

explored surf destination, so get searching…

1 Tynemouth – Longsands beach has been the starting point for some of the UK's top surfers including Gabe Davies and Sam Lamiroy.

2 South Shields – beach break south of the Tyne.

3 Saltburn – a good place for beginners and intermediates as it is a gently sloping beach and water quality has improved recently. The site of one of the East coast's original surf shops where hire boards and wetsuits are available.

4 Whitby – the beach break at Sandsend is a good

spot for more experienced surfers while Whitby beach is good for beginners.

5 Scarborough – the busiest surfing beaches on the east coast. North Bay is a large beach with a sea wall, South Bay is more protected and therefore popular in big storms, and Cayton Bay has a number of breaks suitable for beginners to advanced.

6 East Anglia – look out for a good northerly swell, then head for East Runton and Cromer, which should have good waves for beginners and intermediates.

South Wales

Wales has one of the UK's strongest surf communities and has produced some top international surfer's including former world tour surfer **Carwyn Williams** and up-and-coming shortboarder **Nathan Phillips**. South Wales works well when the cold north-easterly winds blow offshore so a warm wetsuit and strong disposition are needed.

Swansea:

1 Langland Bay – a number of spots in Langland Bay break at various stages of the tide. Beginners should stick to the sandy beach.

2 Oxwich Bay and Horton – both a bit more sheltered and so good spots for beginners.

3 Llangennith – a very long beach which is good for beginners and intermediates when small. The gradual slope of the beach means that the waves are less powerful. But once the swell picks up it's time to head for a more sheltered beach. The Gower is also home to a number of high quality secret spots, which will need skill in both finding and surfing.

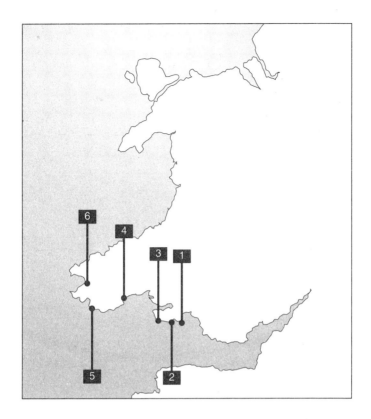

4 Tenby – this sheltered spot breaks in big westerly storm swells, as does Freshwater East.

5 Freshwater West – a long sandy beach that picks up lots of swell and can be a great place for beginners and experienced surfers alike.

6 St Brides Bay and Whitesands Bay – to the west of Haverford West these offer some great breaks for surfers of all abilities.

Scotland

Scotland has some of the most beautiful and unspoilt coastline in the UK. The North Shore has only a handful of resident surfers and some of the most amazing

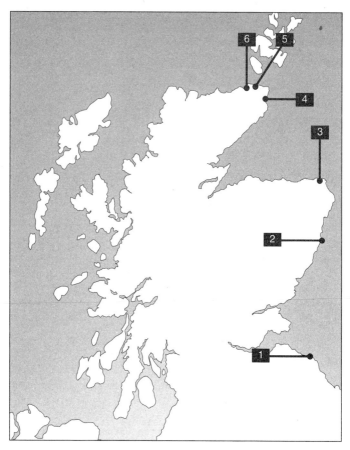

waves to be found in Europe. In the summer it also has the advantage of almost 24 hours of daylight.

1 Pease Bay – a popular spot due to the holiday camp and the easy access from Edinburgh. Peaks at both ends of the bay. Good for beginners and experienced surfers.

2 Aberdeen – Aberdeen has a dedicated group of surfers who brave the cold. Picks up northerly and south-easterly swells.

3 Fraserburgh – probably Scotland's most dedicated surfing community, the area has a number of breaks, including some great beaches for all abilities.

4 Sinclair's Bay – as you head north-east, the number of other surfers decreases. Sinclair's Bay is a very quiet spot, and should only be surfed if you have other experienced surfers with you.

5 Dunnet Bay – also north east, a great spot for beginners as it doesn't handle big swells but is good when small. It's a three-mile-long crescent of sand with a campsite at the eastern end. There are plenty of other spots in the area to progress on to.

6 Thurso East – in the same area, and one of the best reef breaks in Europe. For experienced surfers only, it is a right-hand, flat slate reef that can be either a racing wall or a barrel. If Thurso is a bit beyond your skills, head west to the deserted sandy beaches at Melvich, Strathy, Armadale, Farr Bay or Torrisdale. NEVER surf these spots alone or without an experienced surfer. They can be completely deserted and help may be a while in arriving in the event of a problem. They are also incredibly beautiful and special places to surf where you are regularly accompanied in the line-up by dolphins and seals.

The Channel Islands

Just off the north coast of France, they are a popular holiday destination and pick up westerly swells. Although there are good waves to be found on Guernsey's north-west coast, Jersey is more famed for its surf spots. Check out St Ouen's Bay, a five-mile stretch that has a number of breaks that cater for all abilities.

HOW TO GET AROUND

Feet or two wheels are obviously the best way to hit the

beach but if you can't make it under your own steam, four wheels will do just as well. If you're getting a lift, 'soft racks' are a great investment. These straps secure your boards to the roof without the need of a roof rack and then fold away in your board bag or boot of the car.

TRANSPORT LOTTERY

If you can't blag a lift, you're going to have to go public. This is where you'll run up against rules and regulations. Each train or bus company will have it's own policy on boards so the best advice is check with the line operator.

Trains can be a good way to hit the surf if the break isn't too far from the station or if friends can pick you up. Whether you have to pay to take your board depends on the train company. Be sure to check company policy before you get on the train. The last thing you want is to get stung for extra fares from an over enthusiastic ticket inspector. GNER recommends that you give them a few days' notice when booking your ticket. They will try to accommodate your board in the guard's van and there shouldn't be a charge for it. SWT says boards are carried, 'at the guard's discretion'. If you travel off-peak with SWT it will be easier for them to accommodate your board. However there may be a charge, but no more than £5 each way.

Again buses and coaches are a game of chance and it seems to be left up to the driver to decide. Local buses may take you and your board if the bus is not full and your board isn't massive. However, some bus companies may simply refuse. Coach companies, like National Express state that in theory the coach will carry your board, but again the driver has

Big-wave charger Brock Little drops in at twenty foot Mavericks. The length of his big-wave 'gun' helps him to paddle into these monster waves.

Mark Phipps with a shelf full of blanks waiting to be turned into precision surfboards. This is how all boards start life.

A tail slide is a great addition to any surfer's arsenal – it looks impressive and kicks up loads of spray too!

Britain's World Tour pro Russell Wint executes a perfect 'floater' under the Nor African sun.

Up and riding at surf school – you never forget your first wave.

Tahitian Vetea David tucks into G-Land for a backhand barrel. A hand on the rail creates extra stability.

Three-time World Champion Tom Curren snapping off the lip at Lafitenia, France. A smooth bottom turn helps generate the speed needed for advanced manoeuvres.

▲ Slater launching his new-skool aerial attack over a close-out section.

Keep your eyes open for any warning signs. If in doubt, don't go out – always ask a more experienced surfer's advice.

▲ Top Hawaiian surfer Megan Abubo carves off the bottom, ready for another explosive manoeuvre.

▲ Chelsea Georgeson from down under shows she's not intimidated by the razor reef below as she tucks into another Tavarua barrel in Fiji.

Megan Abubo snaps off the top as seen from the line-up.

Four-time World Champion Lisa Andersen is regarded as one of the best surfers in the world, male or female.

The mark of a great surfer is the ability to generate speed through the bottom turn for cutting-edge manoeuvres, as demonstrated by Slater's aerial.

Beginners in the white water making the most of the off-shore mornings.

Ideal learning conditions – small waves, small crowd, big smile.

Kelly Slater in the barrel in France – roving why he's the six-time surfing World hampion.

Ion Banner bottom turning in the face of a twenty-five foot Mavericks monster.

A Portuguese surfer tucking into a Moroccan barrel.

If you have to surf alone, ensure you surf on a protected beach.

Aussie surfer Mark Bannister demonstrates a classic bottom turn, the key to becoming a good surfer.

▲ Every year the SAS bus tours the UK's coastline with the top international and UK surfers, holding events and raising environmental awareness.

▷ The perfect end to a perfect session. Author Chris Nelson catches the last wave of the day at Morocco's world-famous Ankor Point.

the final say. (The board will be stowed in the hold so pack it well.)

As with other modes of transport, the airlines' rules vary. British Airways recommends that you give your travel agent the weight and dimensions of your board when booking to make sure it will fit on the flight. They will let you know what the extra charge will be as it varies from flight to flight. The same applies to Virgin Airlines. TAP (Air Portugal) doesn't charge for boards at present but make sure you always check before booking. Your board will be part of your weight allowance when you fly with Ryan Air. Claiming for any damage done to your board while in transit with airlines will be limited to a measly $20 per kilo checked in so make sure your travel insurance covers it!

Board bags

Although your pride and joy may seem quite strong, it is actually quite fragile. The glass can easily be punctured by sharp objects; anything heavy placed on them can cause pressure dings and if it is not packed properly your thruster may turn out a twin-fin. Also, if a board is left in the hot sun, it will soon go from pearl white to tea-stained brown. And nothing's worse than getting melted wax over your clothes or your mum's car!

There are a number of types of board bag on the market. A 'board sock', costing around £20, is an elasticated cloth cover that stops you getting wax everywhere and keeps some of the sun off your stick. It doesn't offer any real protection – for this you will need a 'board bag'. These padded bags come in various materials, thicknesses and sizes. Some are designed for heading down the beach, others for the rigours of world travel. 'Coffins' are designed for surfers who want to take a number of boards on a trip and some can carry a full quiver of seven or eight boards! Costing upwards of around £40, there are several good brands to look out for including Rhino and FCS – it's best to talk to your local surf shop about a bag to suit your needs.

If you are packing your board for an overseas trip, make sure it has extra padding to help protect it. Bubble wrap is a great packing material to cover your board before it goes in your board bag. Protect noses, tails and fins with either polystyrene or T-shirts. Unpacking your board to find the nose broken off isn't the best start to a holiday!

EUROPE'S TOP SPOTS

Your first foreign surf trip is something you will never forget. Tackling waves in warm water, at a new break, in a new land, is what surfing is all about. Europe has some of the best waves on the planet and nothing in the world beats sitting on a sand dune in Hossegor after surfing all morning and eating a fresh baguette with some runny Brie. So when the time comes to choose your holiday destination, try steering your family in these directions.

1 Hossegor on France's south-west coast is the most famous beach break in the surfing world. The summer and early autumn mean smaller waves and water warm enough to surf in shorts. Unfortunately it can also get crowded, but you may find yourself sharing a peak with the best surfers in the world. When the

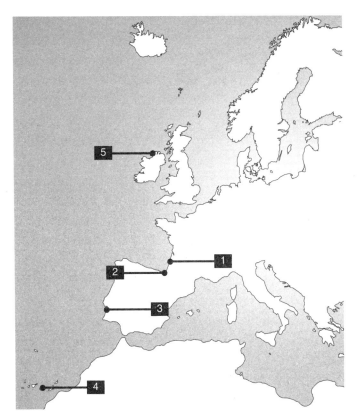

world tour hits Europe all the pros will be there. WCT surfer Damian Hobgood from Florida sums it up well. **'In Hossegor, wherever you get sand bars you and your buddies can have some real fun. You can just sit on the beach all day and enjoy the beach lifestyle.'** As you become a more experienced surfer, you'll want to hit this coastline in spring and autumn as the low pressures in the Atlantic cause bigger swells and more dramatic waves.

2 'Mundaka is a special wave,' explains European champion and Basque surfer **Eneko Acero**. **'I love to surf there because it is such a beautiful place and you can get the**

longest barrels of your life! On a good day you can have half the WCT and WQS surfers in the line-up, but not many will take waves from the locals!' In the Basque region of Northern Spain this river mouth is hailed as one of the longest lefts in Europe and is not a place for inexperienced surfers. It is very powerful, very shallow and very busy. If you are a good surfer there is still the chance of picking up the odd wave, and any wave at Mundaka will be one you'll remember. It needs a big swell to break and works best in spring and also in the autumn – when they hold the WCT contest.

3 In **Portugal** there are some world-class breaks on the west coast near Peniche, Ericiera and Lisbon. As with south west France, Portugal has smaller waves in the summer and bigger swells in the autumn and spring. The winter can be stormy and windy. If you are a young or intermediate surfer, the waves of the Algarve are a great place to head for as it has good weather and good waves all year round. As Toby of 'The Surf Experience' surf camp in Lagos explains, **'There are waves here to suit all abilities and all tastes. Great reefs, great beaches and it gets a lot of swell. If it's too big on the west coast, you can head for the south coast. And it gets more sunshine than anywhere else in Europe!'** WQS surfer **Marlon Lipke** really rates the Algarve. **'The south of Portugal is my favourite place. Zavial and Arrifana are both great waves.'**
4 Gabe Davies describes the **Canary Islands** as 'a great tropical escape in the winter'. A top spot for good

and intermediate surfers, the Canary Islands are a big winter destination due to the warm weather and good swells. While Lanzarote is famed for its big waves, the most popular island with British surfers is Fuerteventura. Unfortunately the Canaries are also a good place to witness the ugly side of surfing, and with its heavy localism, certain areas are best avoided.

5 Some of Europe's best waves can be found closer to home than you think. The west coast of **Ireland** is home to waves that rival Hawaii and Australia. From Bundoran to Easky and down past Spanish Point, with a good map and a sturdy car, you can find enough waves to satisfy even the thirstiest surfer.

European surf camps

If it's your first trip to European waves, why not think about a surf camp? Good surf camps will pick you up from the airport, provide accommodation and food, take you to suitable breaks and some even give you lessons and provide boards and wetsuits. But remember to check that the people running the camps are well qualified in terms of water safety and lifesaving. Check out the Internet and the surf magazines to find what's best for you.

WORLDWIDE

Once you have tasted the thrill of surf travel a whole world of possibilities will be opened up to you. We could fill a library of books talking about all the surf breaks out there, but here are a few names to get you thinking…

1 In the **USA**, the West Coast boasts many legendary breaks. Rincon, Malibu, the Ranch, Santa Cruz, Lower Trestles and Mavericks are all waves that have helped shape the sport. On the east coast Florida's Sebastian Inlet has bred many world-class surfers including Kelly Slater and Lisa Andersen and the Outer Banks have been the scene of many classic sessions.

2 Moving south the Baja peninsular in **Mexico** has traditionally drawn America's best surfers searching for classic empty waves.

3 Further south Puerto Escondido has some of the best beach break barrels in the world. Off the Mexican coast the Island of Todos Santos is home to Killers, one of the planet's few big-wave spots.

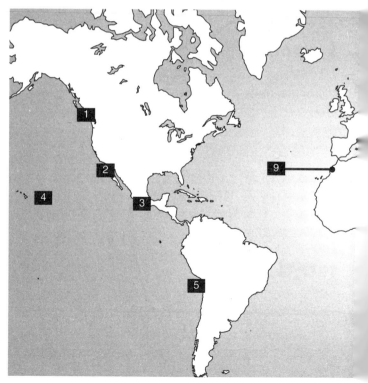

4 Hawaii is the first name that crops up in people's minds when surfing is mentioned. It is where the sport began and it is its spiritual home. The north shore of Oahu is home to the most famous breaks in surfing. Pipeline, Sunset Beach, Waimea and Makaha are known in all corners of the world. However, world class surf can be found on all the Hawaiian Islands. On Maui the monstrous waves at Jaws spawned tow-in surfing and Honalua Bay is a spectacularly long, barrelling right-hander.

5 In South America, **Chile** and **Peru** are both home to classic point breaks with Chicama believed to be the longest wave in the world.

6 Australia is a continent that is always associated

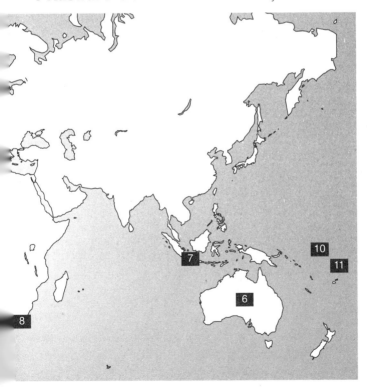

with wave riding and for good reason. From Burleigh Heads, Lennox Head, Kirra and Noosa in the east to Bells Beach and the shark-infested Cactus in the south to Margaret River in the west, Australia has it all.

7 Head north from Australia and you hit **Indonesia**, famed for its warm water and perfect barrels. Uluwatu and Padang Padang on Bali and the straits in Java, peels the world-famous G-Land. Nias, Sumatra, Lombok, Sumbawa and the Mentawai islands are all home to countless waves whose names bring home thoughts of perfect crystal barrels.

8 South Africa has a reputation for big waves and big sharks. From the endless walls of Jeffrey's Bay to the isolation of Breezy Point, South Africa is home to some of the best point breaks on the planet. The Crayfish Factory is as famed for its big waves as Cave Rock is for its barrels.

9 In North Africa, **Morocco**'s famous point breaks have been calling the world's best surfers since the 1970s. Anka Point, Killer Point and Desert Point are all worldclass rights within a short flight from Europe. Every year surfers pack their camper vans and drive down for the warm winter season in Taghazoute.

Pacific islands and island chains are a wave rider's dream.

10 Fiji with Tavarua's Cloudbreak and

11 Tahiti with the incredible and fearsome Teahupoo, are just the tip of a massive iceberg.

It may seem weird and wonderful to find good surf in Japan, Norway, The Caribbean or the Philippines, but scratch the surface and you'll find surfers everywhere, sometimes in the most unexpected places. So the next time you're in the Mediterranean on holiday, just keep an eye on the water.

TOP TRAVEL TIPS FROM THE PROS

The life of a surf pro is an endless journey from contest to contest – today America, tomorrow Japan, next week South Africa. So who better to pass on a few top travel tips for your surf holiday?

As up-and-coming Aussie pro **Jock Barnes** explains, choosing who you go with is the first thing to think about. **'One of the major things is picking the right person to travel with. You're going to be in cars and accommodation with the same people for a long time and travelling with the wrong person can be a bit taxing!'**

Germany's Marlon Lipke competes on the WQS and he reckons organization will make the whole journey easier. **'Three days before you go, write down a list of passports, tickets and things you'll need. Then tick it all off, because if you leave it to the day you go your head will be full of too many things.'**

WCT surfer **Pat O'Connell** from the USA starred in the surf travel film *Endless Summer 2*. As someone who has travelled the whole globe, Pat thinks travelling light is the key. **'The main thing I've learned these past years is not to bring too much stuff. The first time I came to Europe I brought almost everything I owned. Most places have the same things as back home if you forget something, so focus on the basics and you'll be sweet.'**

When you are in a foreign country always remember to respect local customs and traditions. **'When you're travelling always be open-minded,'** recommends top Hawaiian surfer Fred Patacchia, **'because a lot of cultures are different. Like in France they take a long time over dinner. You can't get impatient and bothered by it because it's their way of life.'**

Wherever you go treat the beach as you would your own. **'Be respectful to other people and don't drop any litter,'** says Cornish Open champion Sarah Bentley. **'As the guys at SAS say – "Leave nothing on the beach except footprints!"'**

But the main thing about travel is making the most of the experience. **'Enjoy it as much as possible because travelling and surfing is the best thing you can do,'** says top surfer Tiago Pires from Portugal. **'Travel as much as possible and you'll meet all kinds of people and it will make you appreciate where you are in the world and where you come from.'**

6
Environment

WHAT IS THE ENVIRONMENT?

You may have heard the expression **'I feel like I'm living in a goldfish bowl!'** Well, in a way we are. The planet is like a huge bowl – whatever we do within it is contained and will have an effect on everyone's lives. So we need to make sure that we keep our bowl clean and a nice safe environment to live in.

The word environment is used a lot but what exactly is it?

'The environment is made up of everything that surrounds you and everything that you interact with,' says Sarah Bentley. **'Your house, your friends, the air you breathe, your school, the water you drink, where you play soccer, your local beach – in fact everywhere you go and the things you see, this is your environment. You are part of and everything you do will have an effect on it.'**

Who's out in the line-up with you?

Well, if you've been to the beach, you'll know that the coastal environment is 'diverse' with lots of plants, fish, birds and other animals living in it. Just because you may not see them, it doesn't mean that they aren't there. All around our coastline you can find seal populations. The best places to see them are Scotland, the east coast of

England, Wales, Devon and Cornwall. The common and grey seal are pretty inquisitive mammals and will often approach surfers in the water to check them out. If you see seals on the beach or soaking up some sunshine on the rocks it's best to give them a bit of space as they can give you a nasty nip if they get scared.

Don't panic if you see a fin lurking in the British waters – 99 per cent of the time it will be a dolphin. The other 1 per cent will usually be something equally harmless, like a porpoise, whale or basking shark. Dolphins are believed to be one of the planet's most intelligent creatures. Travelling together in groups called pods, these playful mammals may also approach surfers. As dolphins are big fans of surfing and playing in waves, good places to catch a glimpse of them on a clear glassy day are Cornwall, Scotland and Wales.

Porpoises are smaller relatives of dolphins and spend most of their time hunting further out at sea, so you might need your binoculars to spot them.

If you are very lucky you may see either a basking shark or whales. Although basking sharks are the second biggest species of shark in the world, there is no need to be afraid of this gentle giant. It feeds in the same way as many species of whale – by filtering plankton out of the water – so not only are they toothless, they are also pretty 'armless. (Sorry!) These incredible creatures were hunted nearly to the point of extinction so are now quite rare in our waters. Various species of whales can also be seen in the waters around the UK. A great place to spot them is off the north coast of Scotland where they navigate between the main land and the Orkney Isles, which were even named after the orca or killer whales. You will need a good pair of binoculars and a very calm day but you may see minke whales, sperm whales, pilot whales or even killer whales which, despite their 'fright night' name, have never been known to attack humans. Even if you don't live in any of the areas listed, keep your eyes open as these marine mammals can crop up anywhere along Britain's coastline.

While in the line-up, you will often see fish such as salmon jumping out of the water. Sometimes they are doing this to avoid predators, such as seals or other fish. Raining down like bombs, big groups of diving birds like gannets or cormorants will often show you where there is a big shoal of fish. In fact fishermen have followed diving birds for years to find a fish-rich spot to lay their nets.

Sometimes the sea will be peppered with a beautiful array of jellyfish, which don't swim but are carried by the currents. Waves approaching the peak may have fish such as bass or mullet swimming through the face and overhead puffins may be ferrying an endless supply of fish back to hungry chicks.

All you have to do is to keep your eyes and your mind open and you'll be amazed at exactly who you're sharing your surf session with.

WHAT A WASTE

Most of the products your household buys in its weekly shop goes into the bin when they're finished. Some substances, such as bleaches and disinfectants, are designed to be poured down the sink or toilet. These products all go into the environment. They fall into two categories: biodegradable materials such as paper packaging, waste food, certain chemicals, etc will eventually 'break down' in the environment, non-biodegradable waste such as plastics, metals and certain chemicals will stay in the environment. Both can cause pollution, look and smell bad and affect other lives on the planet. Dolphins can get caught up in discarded fishing nets, seals can get snared by the looped plastic packaging that holds cans of drink together or you could even tread on a rusty can washed on to the shore.

Next time you think recycling is too much trouble, think about the fact that we are still digging Roman coins, glassware and even leather sandals out of the ground. Imagine how long it will take for a plastic bottle to break down. It may still be here in thousands of years! Is this the way you want our civilisation remembered?

Pollution and sewage

Unfortunately, for years the ocean has been seen as a convenient place to dispose of waste. It was thought that it was so huge that pollution would just disappear. We now know that this is not true. Everything we put into the environment has an effect, no matter how small.

Sewage is made up of everything that goes down the toilet (you know what we mean) and waste from sinks. At bathing beaches sewage outfalls should at least have had some basic processing before being dumped into the sea, but for years raw sewage was dumped into the water all around the country. This situation has now improved to the point where the quality at many bathing beaches is much better. But surf breaks aren't just found on bathing beaches.

'Porthleven is probably regarded as one of

the best breaks in the UK,' says James Hendy of environmental group Surfers Against Sewage, **'but it's a reef right next to the harbour. No one ever goes swimming there so it's not classed as a bathing area. Because of this it's not tested for water quality and it is not subject to any pollution control.'** Some surf breaks are still very polluted by sewage.

Pollution is anything introduced into the environment that disrupts the natural balance. It could be noise pollution from a major road, thermal pollution (waste heat) from power stations, or chemicals dumped into the sea. Whether deliberate or an accident, it is still a problem.

Effects from pollution can be immediate and attract a lot of attention, for instance when an oil tanker sinks. But it can also be a gradual thing. If factories are discharging waste into the sea, species of fish may become sick and gradually disappear. Some pollution can be invisible. Sandside Bay in Scotland is one of the best surf breaks in Caithness. Unfortunately it is near Dounreay Nuclear Power Plant. Signs on the beach warn of radioactive particles and the dangers of playing in the sand. How safe would it be to surf there?

ENVIRONMENTAL ORGANIZATIONS

Some people feel so strongly about the damage being done to the environment that they have formed proactive groups to do something about it.

Surfing organizations

Surfers Against Sewage is a very successful environmental group formed by a band of surfers from the Cornish vil-

lage of St Agnes. Upset by the polluted state of the water they decided, rather than just moan, to take action. **'We started back in 1990 because we were getting ill from surfing our local beaches,'** explained James Hendy. **'People were getting ear, nose and throat infections, stomach upsets – diarrhoea, vomiting, and we were just tired of getting sick. I was introduced to surfing by my dad and the thing about surfing is that it is a great sport to keep you fit and you're also feeding off the energy of Mother Nature. All surfers are naturally environmentalists because they are using the environment the whole time.**

'Originally all we wanted to do was to clean up our three beaches – Porthtowan, St Agnes and Perranporth. I remember coming out of the water and seeing maggots on the shoreline and thinking it had got too bad to ignore. By 1994 we had nearly 15,000 members.

'It's come a long way,' says James, **'but only really because they have upgraded a lot of the old water treatment works through pressure from people like Surfers Against Sewage.'**

Today, SAS is a national organization and is backed by many top national and international surf stars, such as Masters Champion **Gary Elkerton**. Each year the SAS team and top pros travel nationwide on the SAS Tour Bus, hosting talks and competitions and raising awareness about the environment.

Surfrider Foundation was formed in America in the

1984 and is now the world's largest grass roots environmental group. The strength of the group is that it has a network of local 'chapters' which work at a local level. They've sued polluters through the court system as well as initiating a system of water testing that the US government themselves refused. In 1990 top surfer Tom Curren opened a European chapter. Check them out on www.surfrider-europe.org

Marine Conservation Society

The MCS run some excellent schemes including Adopt a Beach and Beach Watch. They also do beach clean-ups and have a really useful *Good Beach Guide*, www.goodbeachguide.co.uk. Check out their website to see what you can do to be involved on www.mcsuk.org

Quiksilver Initiative and The Crossing

The Initiative and *The Crossing* are aimed at raising environmental issues at a global and local level as well as gathering data to find out how pollution has impacted on the environment. As Caroline Whalley, European Water Check Supervisor, on Quiksilver's *The Crossing* says **'We need to be monitoring all year round. We have wetsuits now that mean we can be in the water for up to three hours in the winter. If treatment facilities are being turned off outside the traditional summer bathing time then we are not all being protected.'**

WHAT CAN I DO?

Well, the simple answer is 'a lot'! **'If people think**

when they are in the supermarket, buying products for the house, that is where it starts,' explains James. **'Hassle your parents to buy environmentally sound products – detergents, dishwashing liquid, etc. It's all out there to use. The water industry has to clean up our waste water and if people start using more environmentally friendly products in the households it would help them deal with all these products.'**

'One of our major campaign slogans is "Bag it, bin it." Sanitary products such as tampons and sanitary towels have got to be put in a bag and then in the bin. Don't put them down the toilet. Treatment plants can get blocked up with sanitary products. I've been surfing and seen things like nappies float past! It's incredible that someone has just thought "I'll put that down the toilet." 75 per cent of beach litter according to a recent survey, was made up of cotton buds. The little plastic sticks flushed down the toilet end up on the beach. If people buy paper ones or put them in the bin, that's a big help. Once people start using environmentally friendly products and disposing of things properly, more of their friends will.'

Another way you can help is by organizing a clean-up at your local beach. With a group of friends, surf club or Scouts or Guides, collect all the litter and rubbish you find on the beach. **'We can help advise you how to organize a clean up,'** says James, **'what to pick up and more importantly what not to**

pick up on the beach. If you contact us or the Marine Conservation Society, we will give you a checklist of what to avoid. Also make sure there's an adult with you, always wear gloves and count the number of things you pick up as SAS keep a record.' If you need any help in organizing a beach clean-up contact SAS through their website: www.sas.org.uk. SAS have also put together a learning package for schools, so ask your teacher to get in touch and educate your class-mates.

Caroline Whalley says **'Anyone who has ever been ill after being in the water should con-tact SAS. They have a medical data base and they can use these statistics as a weapon in their campaign. People need to be careful when disposing of motor oil, and conscious of what they put down the toilet, such as plastics. It all gets out to sea eventually, so look after your environment. Remember, don't destroy what you came to enjoy!'**

7
Where do waves come from?

'You're never going to be able to master the ocean. That's the hardest thing about surfing. You've got tennis players out there who can nail it because they're playing on something that never changes. With surfing you never know when the next wave's going to break or how big it will be. You don't even know if you're going to catch a wave.'
Jock Barnes, professional surfer.

The football pitch has gone!

Imagine if you turned up to play soccer and found the pitch had disappeared. Imagine trying to play golf on a green where the grass is long one second and short the next, or where the hole is constantly moving. Well that's what surfing is like. The wind can suddenly shift blowing the waves out, the swell can drop in minutes, the tide can cause a perfect peak to become white-water slop. No two waves are ever the same. But there is a reason why the waves were lined-up corduroy yesterday but are choppy today. To unlock these secrets, you must first learn about the weather.

Why the weatherman is your new best friend!

To a surfer the weather forecast is the most important TV programme of the day. If you know what to look for, it can tell you exactly where and when there will be waves. It can make the difference between a long and fruitless journey to the coast or scoring perfect waves before the crowds have heard about the new swell.

WHERE DO WAVES COME FROM?

To understand how to predict waves, you need to take a look at where wind comes from, as it is wind that creates waves.

Low pressures

You might hear a surfer at the beach saying the following: **'There's a deep low in the slot so I reckon it's gonna be going off on Friday at low tide.'** But what does that mean?

OK, this will seem like a science lesson, but bear with it and the secrets of surfing will be revealed – plus you'll be able to impress your mates with your surf predictions and forecasts!

The earth's atmosphere is made up of a huge layer of gas, just as the oceans are made up of a huge layer of water. It operates in exactly the same way as the oceans in that it has vast currents or 'winds'. Winds are caused when air moves from an area where there is 'more air' (high pressure) to an area where there is 'less air' (low pressure or a depression). Low pressure systems are called depressions because they are like valleys in the atmosphere. The column of air above that part of the world is shallower. A high pressure on the other hand, is like a 'hill' of air. Because the column of air in that area is taller, it creates a higher pressure at ground level (just as deeper water exerts more pressure). The atmosphere, like the ocean, likes to have everything in balance. So air moves from the high pressure to the low pressure, which slowly fills up until it disappears. This movement of air is the wind.

The wind spirals into a low pressure like water moving down the plughole – in the northern hemisphere it spirals in an anti-clockwise direction and in the southern hemisphere it turns the other way.

Where do the swells come from?

As the wind travels across the surface of the oceans it creates a 'swell'. The friction of the wind on the surface of the ocean pushes the water, creating ripples. For surfers to get good waves a number of factors need to occur. The wind needs to be over a certain strength, usually 20 or 25mph. It needs to blow in a particular direction over a long area or 'fetch'. The stronger the winds and the longer the fetch, the bigger the waves will be.

There are different types of swell caused by low pressures. The first type is called a 'wind swell'. This occurs close to, or in the area where the wind is blowing. The waves are usually small, close together and weak. The swell is choppy and 'confused'. However, as the swell moves further away from the low pressure it becomes organized into a 'ground swell'. If you look out to sea from a headland you can see the neat lines of a

ground swell marching in. This is sometimes referred to as 'corduroy'.

Waves in a ground swell become bigger and cleaner and form 'sets'. Sets are regular groups of waves that are bigger than the waves in-between.

Surfers look for a number of things when they study the weather: low pressure that is 'deep' enough to generate strong winds (usually below 996mb), far enough away to smooth it into a good ground swell (a couple of days) and one that will blow long enough to create good conditions for a few days. If a low pressure is 'in the slot', it is in the perfect position to produce waves for a particular area.

If a surfer can read a chart well, they may travel to the other side of the country, arrive when the surf is flat, and know that when they wake up in the morning it will be perfect.

Tides and swell – the key to surf forecasting

Just turning up at a beach when a good swell is expected doesn't mean you'll get good waves. What happens when the swell arrives is just as important.

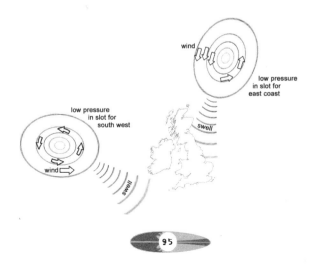

WHEN THE SWELL HITS

When you watch surf videos, or travel around, you will notice that waves from different breaks have very different characteristics. Some waves are very fast and hollow. Others may be slow-peeling and not very steep. Some waves are very long, while others may be short but sweet. But what causes these differences and why is it important to know your 'points' from your 'peaks'?

Why does a wave break?

As a peak, or wave, approaches the land, the sea becomes shallower. The bottom of the wave begins to feel resistance from the sea floor, effectively dragging it along, causing the bottom of the wave to slow down. The shallower water causes the wave to grow in height and at the same time friction from the seabed slows the bottom of the wave down even more. The top of the wave is now travelling faster than the bottom and the wave falls forward, breaking.

Imagine a group of stuntmen on motorcycles, riding around a field. Standing on their shoulders is a human pyramid of performers. The taller the human pyramid, the more unstable it becomes. If the motorcycles stop suddenly, the pyramid will fall forward.

How big is that wave?

Measuring wave height may seem like a mystery. It looks head high with a 6ft surfer riding it, but you're told by a local it's only 4ft. The other day it was shoulder high but they said it was 3ft. What does this all mean? Did they miss maths lessons? Well, in surfing the swell is measured rather than the waves. A wave face may be eight feet, but the swell may only be 5 or 6 ft. As mentioned, waves jack up when they hit the beach and the same swell may produce different size wave faces at different breaks. So when you talk about wave faces it may be head-high, but the swell may only be 4ft.

Wave peaking

Wave breaking

Why do waves break differently?

There are many factors that affect how a wave breaks

when it finally reaches land. If just one of these factors is wrong then the quality of the wave may be ruined.

a. The swell's characteristics

If a swell travels a long way, it will be clean and lined up when it hits. But the size of the swell also has a major effect on the wave quality. Some breaks can't handle waves over a certain size and may no longer 'peel' and simply 'close out'. Check your break in different swells to see how it works.

b. Local conditions
Tides and the moon

Tides are very important to surfers as certain surf spots only break at certain 'states of tide' – low tide, mid tide

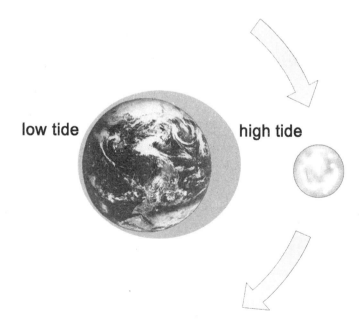

low tide   high tide

or high tide. Tides are caused by the movement of the moon as it revolves around the earth. Just as the earth has a gravitational pull, which keeps us from floating off into space, so does the moon. Although it is weaker than the earth's gravity, it is strong enough to pull the oceans towards the moon.

As the moon reaches the other side of the globe it pulls the water towards it, creating a low tide on this side of the world. The same happens in reverse at high tide when the moon is nearest to us, pulling the water to this side of the planet.

Pick up a copy of the *Tide Tables* for your surfing area from surf or fishing shops or tourist information offices. They're free and will tell you the tides for the whole year.

Some breaks, such as river mouths, may be affected by currents triggered by tidal changes. A break that may be safe on an incoming tide may develop dangerous rips when the tide starts to go out, so it's important to learn about a new break before you surf it.

Wind

Local conditions, like wind, may suddenly change from a perfect 'offshore' – blowing out to sea and giving the waves a good shape – to a mushy 'onshore' direction. Onshore winds cause waves to lose their shape, break irregularly and become lumpy. A perfect swell that has travelled thousands of miles can be ruined by a change of wind direction on the beach.

N.B. Swell and wind directions are based on the direction they come from. A north-easterly wind comes from the north-east. It is the same with swell direction.

A south-westerly swell comes from the south-west.

c. The shape of the sea bed

What a wave looks like is mainly determined by the shape of the sea bed where it breaks. A wave hitting a suddenly steep sand bank or reef may 'throw over' into a barrel. The sudden change of depth causes the lip to form a hollow wave. This can happen on a sandy bottom like Hossegor in France, or on a reef bottom such as Pipeline in Hawaii. If the change is more gradual, then the wave may not have the energy to form a barrel and may become a peeling wall. If a beach has a very gradual slope the waves simply crumble. These waves are best for learning on – leave the barrels to the experienced surfers.

d. What the sea bed is made of

Surfers may prefer a **reef** or a sandbar depending upon their ability or confidence levels.

A reef is solid and made of boulders, rock or coral, so does not move. Waves will always break on a reef in the same place. A good reef set-up usually has a 'channel' (area where the waves aren't breaking) out to the peak. This means avoiding the need for a massive duck diving session. Reefs are not recommended for beginners as they do not make for a soft landing. Famous reefs include Scotland's Thurso East, Tahiti's infamous Teahupoo and Indonesian gem G-Land.

Sand banks can have just as good a shape and size as a reef, but may not be a permanent fixture. Sandbars can arrive and be gone within a few weeks. Hitting a sand bottom can still lead to injuries but is less dangerous than hitting sharp rocks. A drawback to surfing a beach is that there may not be very clear channels to get out the back in bigger surf, so this is where your duck-diving skills really come into play. Famous beach breaks include Cornwall's Fistral Beach, Supertubes in Portugal and Puerto Escondido in Mexico.

A **point break** is, as it sounds, a wave that peels along a point of land, finger of land or a headland. Point breaks are characteristically quite long waves. Famous points include Californian waves Rincon and Malibu, Australia's Kirra, Anka Point in Morocco and Lafitenia in south-west France.

River mouth breaks occur where silt or sand has been deposited by a river when it reaches the sea and has built up into a long sandbar. Waves will characteristically peel along the sandbar away from the river mouth. Famous river mouth breaks include Torrisdale in Scotland and Mundaka in the Basque region of Spain – one of the longest waves in Europe and the world's most famous river mouth.

Peaks, lefts and rights

One thing that confuses non-surfers and beginners alike is whether a wave is peeling right or left. It might look like it should be a left, but in fact it's a right. Why? The direction of a wave is decided not by the way the wave peels when looked at from the shore, but from the way the wave is peeling when you are riding it. So a wave you go right on is a right-hander, though when watched from the beach it will seem to be peeling left. Say this fast and it will confuse everyone, but a regular footer will ride a right, facing the wave, and a goofy footer will ride backhand. Famous rights include Thurso East, Bell's Beach

A 'left'

A 'right'

A 'peak'

in Australia, Jeffries Bay in South Africa and Sunset Beach in Hawaii.

A left is ridden by a regular footer on their backhand; a goofy will be forehand or facing the wave. Famous lefts include Pipeline, Mundaka, Tavarua in Fiji and Chicama in Peru.

A peak can be a reef or a sandbar that has waves that travel both left and right. It produces a 'peak' in the middle, from where a surfer can go in either direction. You may hear the phrase 'It had perfect peaks all the way along it!' used to describe a good beach.

HOW TO CHECK THE SURF

The more you surf, the more you can see how different conditions affect different spots. You can also try your hand at forecasting when the waves will be good. But if you haven't mastered the finer points of swell prediction, don't worry. There are plenty of other ways to find out if the swell's hit or is on its way.

Surf shops that are on or near the sea front usually don't mind telling you what the surf is like, especially if you are a regular customer. Just remember that they also have a business to run, so don't go ringing five or six times a day.

Ceefax has surf pages currently on BBC page 429. These include surf reports from various locations around the UK and some surf news.

Internet/webcams have become a valuable resource for surfers wanting to find out when the swell's going to hit. There are many sites with swell predictions for all parts of the world. Check out www.surfersvillage.com and go from there.

Text messages – It's Going Off is a surf information

service providing surf forecasts, beach checks and wave buoy data direct to your mobile phone. You select your favourite break and they'll give you regular reports. A great service – but it does cost money to use. (www.itsgoingoff.com)

Surf lines have been around for years and these 0898 type premium rate numbers aren't the cheapest way to find out what's happening. Last resort.

Friends by the sea are by far the cheapest and easiest way of finding out how the surf is. If you haven't made friends with local surfers yet, now's the time.

8
Clubs

Joining a club is one of the best ways to meet other surfers in your area, and introduce you to a whole new group of friends.

The biggest club in the UK is the BSA or British Surfing Association. Becoming a member of this national organization will mean you can get discounted lessons at the BSA's National Surfing Centre and when you progress, you can take part in BSA contests. If you are good enough, you may even be considered to represent your country as part of the British Surf Team. As a member you'll be insured for third party liability, just in case you injure someone else while you're tearing it up in the water. You will also be sent their newsletter three times a year as well as the annual BSA handbook, which contains, among other things, a listing of local surf clubs across the country. If you're interested in joining up or just finding out more about the BSA and other local clubs near you, log on to www.britsurf.co.uk or email karen@britsurf.co.uk

If you live in Wales, then check out the WSF. Similar to the BSA, the Welsh Surfing Federation is responsible for running the Welsh National Championships and selecting the teams to represent Wales at international events. As well as running a surf school at Llangennith Beach, they also run a number of contests throughout the year, for which you'll need to be a member to take part. Local club contacts can be found on the website www.welshsurfingfederation.co.uk. As WSF secretary, Lynda Keward explains, **'These clubs offer more than just surfing, they hold coaching sessions, run small contests, social events and trips.'** So go on, what are you waiting for?

If you can't find a club in your area, why not set up your own? Get a group of friends together and off you go. Get a good name and organize monthly meets and informal contests. It's a great way to meet new people, helping each other out with advice, equipment and lifts to the beach. If you want to make the club more official, you'll need to rope in a responsible adult – a teacher or someone's parent – who can help you with running the club smoothly, with things such as money-raising and approaching businesses for prizes. If you need advice on setting up an official club, why not contact the BSA or WSF?

9
Lifestyle

SURF CULTURE

We're a pretty unique breed of people, surfers. Apart from fishermen and farmers, who do you know who takes an interest in the five-day weather forecast? We eat, sleep, breathe surfing. So much so that there is a company out there to cater for our every need – from the clothes we wear, to the films we watch, to the books we read, even to the holidays we want to go on. Surfing is more than just riding waves – it's a way of life.

SURF THREADS – HEAD TO TOE

Picture the scene.

It's a hot summer's day and you and your mates are heading down to the beach for some serious surf action. You scoop your board up under your arm and stroll out of the door. As you walk down the road, people stop dead in their tracks and turn to stare. Coming towards you is that certain someone you've been trying to impress all summer. As they get closer they begin to laugh and look away. Then, horror of horrors, you catch sight of yourself in the shop window. Buckle-up sandals with socks, checked 'hammer pants', a neon green rash vest, topped off with a *Little House on the Prairie*-style bandanna. Aaaarggghhh!!!

You wake up and realize it was only a dream or, more accurately, a nightmare – this time.

So you've got the board, had the lessons and now you want to get the T-shirt. But where do you head to make sure you don't commit the fashion crime of the century? And what are the rules of looking like a surfer? Well the honest answer is, there are no rules. Surfing is an individual sport. It's all about expression both in and out of the water and there are as many surf looks as there are styles of riding – longboarding, shortboarding, minimal riding, new skool, old skool – you get the picture. There are however, lines that should not be crossed!

Top British surfer Sam Lamiroy recalls one incident that resulted in a drastic change of image. **'I was out surfing in France and there was this pro contest on and this guy says to me "You surf really well, you should be in the contest." I said I was only 16 and there with some mates, and that I wasn't in the league of the pros. He said "You really should do the contest – you're the best girl surfer I've ever seen!" So long hair can be a danger when you're young and I wouldn't recommend it!'**

Admittedly some people can get away with long-locks – like big-wave charger and *Rolling Thunder* star **Robbie Page** – but it is not essential. In fact nearly all of the top 44 riders have opted for short cuts and some, including Kelly Slater and Russell Winter, look more US marine than 70s' surf scene.

While we're on hair, a word from the wise is to remember to wash the salt out after hitting the surf. **'Dreadlocks were a mistake. They weren't planned – it was just skanky hair,'** confesses former British Champion Gabe Davies. If you do have long hair and can't be tempted into a trip to the hairdresser's, a tip from American longboarder **Missy Gibson** is to **'put olive oil in your hair before you go into the water'.** It coats your hair and stops it getting too tangled up in the sea – just don't use that expensive extra virgin olive oil in the cupboard or your hair will be the last thing you need to worry about!

Getting the look

Rob Pascoe is the General Manager of Quiksilver UK, so he knows what's hot and what's not. In terms of summer, he says, **'For the ultimate surf look I would suggest baseball cap, good backpack, strong printed T-shirt, a good pair of jeans – which is essential, and a real cool pair of skate shoes.'** If you feel confined by wearing shoes in the summer, then stick on a pair of flip-flops. For guys, throw a short-sleeved, print or check shirt over your tee and for girls, you can swap slim fit tees for vest tops. When it's hot, trade jeans for knee-length or 3/4-length shorts or boardies. Girls, mix the look up with a denim knee-length or mini skirt or short shorts and pull on a wide brim 'bush style' sun hat.

The surf look is like any fashion – certain looks have a moment in the sun, then crash and burn. Others, like Hawaiian shirts, keep coming around again. **'There are people out there who like louder clothing,'** says Rob. **'That's where the Hawaiian shirts come in, particularly now with the old-skool Fifties-style prints coming back.'**

For winter, pull a good sweatshirt or hoodie on over the top, swap your cap for a knitted beanie and zip up your parka or snowboarding jacket, which has the added bonus of being water-proof and windproof.

The number one thing to stick on to perfect the surf look is a good waterproof sun block. As a surfer, you spend hours outside and don't want to end up looking like a burnt tourist. Even on days that seem cloudy, you can still get burnt as the sea acts as a massive reflector. So as they say in Australia, the nation of sun and surf – slip, slap, slop!

Who's hot?

The surf look of the moment is influenced by skate, snow and street. So who's hot and who's not? Well, as with all things it's just a matter of taste. Billabong, O'Neill and Quiksilver are the big three of the surfing world. **'Rip Curl is a great brand,'** says Rob. **'The smaller brands like Rusty and Hurley are becoming strong again. Volcom is a big brand in the States.'**

Other surf brands to look at include Gotcha, Headworx and Mambo. Unless you're a sponsored surfer, there's no need to wear one brand top to toe. The key to getting the surf look is to make it your own and mix it up with jean or street brands such as Levis, Diesel, Stussy and Gap. For a surfing new-skool look, add skate tees from smaller labels like Unabomber, Panic or Consolidated or surf companies like Counter Culture and Lost.

The top brand for surf girls is Roxy. Other brands include O'Neill's Board Babes, Billabong Girls and Voo Doo Dolls.

'For girls, the way you wear the look is only limited by your imagination,' says Sarah Bentley, **'so you can mix and match your surf wear with other favourite pieces from your wardrobe. For me, I mainly wear Roxy but you**

can also find some great bargains and belts in **Top Shop, or you can always make your own ...'**

What's not hot?

Boardies are the staple of every surfer's wardrobe. Unfortunately, in the UK and most of Europe, there are very few times when you actually get to surf in them. There is one rule when it comes to surf shorts – elasticated waists are a no-go area. If you do get to surf without a suit, a drawstring or popper will stop you exiting the water minus your shorts after a wipe-out. And trust me, this does happen.

For girls, surfing in a bikini top might not be the best idea – a rash vest will save your modesty and your skin from too much sun. But save your rash vest for the beach only. According to Sarah Bentley, **'One of the worst fashion crimes is wearing your rash vest out to a nightclub. Even worse is wearing those baggy, check trousers that look like pyjamas!'**

Enter one of the best-dressed Brit surfers, Gabe Davies, who confesses to some skeletons in his wardrobe. **'I did have some of those checked 'Hammer' pants and a pink Hot Tuna visor. Sun visors are back in now and I've lost it.'**

The thing with fashion is that it is always changing, and what's 'out' one year is 'in' the next.

Rob Pascoe admits his worst fashion crime still lives in his wardrobe. **'I had – and still have – a Body Glove sweatshirt from 1982 that was the most day-glo, outrageous, multitude of colours, that looks like someone has been ill over it. I thought I was so cool wearing it.'** Who knows, given long enough even that may be the trend again!

Other things to avoid – bandannas, luminous T-shirts (unless you see Kelly Slater or **Keala Kenneley** in them), socks with sandals, ghetto blasters – this isn't Flashdance and you don't want to get sand in your stereo. And the number one thing you should get rid of if you're a surfer is a bad attitude – it's so last year.

What to clothe your feet in?

Well, in the summer you can't beat a good pair of flip-flops for that 'I live at the beach' look. From branded Reefs to 'a pound a pair' from the beach-front shops, anything goes. When not in flip-flops, a good pair of skate shoes is compulsory. The daddy of the skate shoe is Vans, who manage to be both popular and cool with old and new skool surfers. The secret is to get your Vans from a skate shop where they sell a different range from high street outlets. Just as cool as Vans for guys and girls are Etnies, Es and Emerica, Gravis, Globe, Reef and Gallaz (for girls only). Skate shoes can be expensive but you don't have to break the bank. Top tip – check the shops when the new ranges come in as they usually sell off the slightly older styles at a knock-down price. Also cheaper and still cool are 'old skool' classics like Converse All Stars or Dunlop 'Green Flash'.

SURF STUFF

From stickers to bags, surfers like their accessories, but what is the latest 'must have'?

Stickers – Essential and great for customising

your boards, bedroom, school books, etc. Top tip – try writing to your favourite surf brand enclosing an s.a.e. explaining that they are your favourite surf company ever and that you'd love some stickers. If you sound polite/worthy enough, you might be lucky.

Wallets – Well, you're going to need somewhere to stash all those phone numbers! A surf brand wallet is the perfect place.

Key chains – Hang them round your neck for that 'access all areas' look or jam your keys in your pocket with the loop hanging out for a more subtle approach.

Watches – Tide watches are a staple of all surf brands now. At around £80, they are pretty expensive but they will let you know when the tide is just right for that elusive sandbar. Most good surf companies produce them, as do Nixon, Animal and G-Shock. Casio is good for gadgets and has a watch that doubles as a camera – great for taking pictures of your new secret spot.

Sunnies – Every surfer needs to invest in a good pair of sunnies, but they don't have to cost the earth. Make sure that they have decent lenses with UV protection as cheap glasses can damage your eyes. Check out surfwear brands as well as eyewear firms Oakley, Smith, Dragon, Bolle, Black Fly's, Adidas and Arnette.

Backpacks – Another essential item which will double up as a home for books as well as your wetsuit, though not at the same time. Priced from about £30 upwards, you can also look out for alternatives from Da Kine, Eastpak and Karrimor or check out your local army surplus store for a cheaper alternative.

Skateboards – When the surf is flat, which may seem like all the time, it's time to break out the skateboard.

Whether to practice your ollies, or to take your longboard for a carve, skating will definitely help your surfing technique. In fact skating, known as sidewalk surfing, was invented by a group of surfers during a flat spell in 1950s America.

Board racks – Why have your pride and joy hidden away in the garage when it can live on your bedroom wall where you can keep a loving eye on it. Available through surfing mags, or try persuading your dad what a great idea it would be to keep your room tidy.

CD/MP3 player – Essential for those pre-surf blasts to prepare you for the freezing winter water. Casio even makes an MP3 playing watch!

Waterproof camera – To capture your every wave, you can pick up a disposable camera from Boots or Kodak, waterproof to about 10 metres and costing about a tenner. Or you can splash out upwards of £80 for a waterproof compact (more environmentally friendly).

Waterproof video camera – Most of the latest palm-corders have waterproof housings – great for filming the next *Endless Summer* at your local break

Computer Games – When the surf's flat and your spirits are as wet as the weather, practice your manoeuvres with Kelly Slater's *Pro Surfer* or *Tony Hawk's Pro Skater* – you'll soon be back on top form.

These gadgets are great but the best thing about surfing is … all you really need is your board, some waves, your wetsuit and you!

SURF TUNES

Surf music is a broad church. Contrary to what some people believe, surfer's CD players aren't permanently blasting out *Surfin' USA* by the Beach Boys. Every surfer has his or her own musical tastes, whether it's to get them amped up pre-surf or to help them wind down after a long day at the beach. Sam Lamiroy sums it up. **'Some punk's good and I like Red Hot Chilli Peppers, Nirvana, The Pixies and Sublime. Rage Against the Machine are quite full on and that's good for when the waves are big. But my musical taste is quite a varied bag. Even Britney has her moments – just get a selection, get a multi-stack CD player and hit Random.'**

But there are some artists that crop up again and again. Britain's Russell Winter is a fan of Rap and hip-hop. **'I like Ice Cube, Snoop, Eminem, but also funky music like Jamiroquay and Mary J Blige.'** European champion Eneko Acero says, **'I like older bands, like Pearl Jam.'** His brother Kepa has different taste. **'I like more chilled music, like Van Morrison.'** *Endless Summer 2* star and world tour pro Pat O'Connell likes his music to be a bit more chilled as well. **'As far as music goes, I'm really into a girl called Norah Jones. She is awesome and makes mellow beautiful songs.'** For Sarah Bentley, music helps her relax and focus before she hits the water, **'I always surf better when I'm calm, so I put on mellow music like Zero 7 or India Ire.'**

Ben Harper is a favourite with many touring pros like Nathan Hedge, Pancho Sullivan, Chris Davidson and Mick Fanning. Take a look in Shea Lopez's or former world champ Occy's CD box and you'll find they are both big reggae fans.

Surf stars like Kelly Slater, Rob Machado and Peter

King hit the world of music as a rock band called The Surfers. And more recently top surfer, **Jack Johnson** has made a huge impression with his first CD *Brushfire Fairytales* which Sam describes as, **'Really mellow, with kind of an after surf feel about it'.**

But this works both ways – while surfers have been moving into music, musicians have been entering the water. The Red Hot Chilli Peppers, who starred as surf punks in Hollywood film, *Point Break*, are big fans of surfing. As lead singer, Anthony Kiedis explains, **'Nothing feels quite as good as paddling out into the ocean on a surfboard.'** British rock band Reef's music is inspired by their love of surfing and the ocean, while Pearl Jam's lead singer Eddie Vodder seems to have become a regular rider on surf trips with good friend Kelly Slater. But it doesn't stop there – it seems like everyone, from former Wham! star Andrew Ridgely to Perry Farell of Jane's Addiction, enjoys walking the board. You never know who you might meet in the line-up!

SURF MAGS

When it's grey and cold outside there is nothing better than losing yourself in the world of 'the surf mag'. In magazines the sky is always blue, the waves are always perfect, and the person on the page is always you. You see yourself pull into that barrel at Teahupoo, take off on that huge Sunset peak or be towed into that 40ft monster at Jaws. It's surf magazines that fire your imagination and drive your ambition to get back into the water at the first possible chance, even if it's 2ft, cold and raining.

In the UK we are lucky to have a number of boarding magazines including surf magazines *Carve*, *Wavelength*, and *The Surfer's Path*. Once a month you can get your fix of the Newquay based mags, *Carve* and *Wavelength*, which feature UK surfers at home and abroad. They're also good for keeping up to date with all that is happening in the world of surf – competition listings and results, news and reviews of hardware and videos, as well as tips for improving your surfing. Published ten times a year *The Surfer's Path* is more travel-based, with features and writers from around the globe. *Surf Europe* goes out across the continent six times a year during summer months. Featuring surfers and stories from across Europe, it shows the true calibre of surf our continent offers. You can get all these magazines via subscription or through your newsagent, local WHSmith or surf shop.

If you hit the shops, you should also be able to find some good international surfing magazines. *Surfer*, *Surfing* and *Transworld Surf* are American mags and as such mainly feature the US scene, as well as some Australian surfers. They include travel stories and news from the world tour, as well as being a good source of posters for your walls. *Surfing Girl* and *Wahine Magazine* are from the US and *Waves' Surf Girl* and *Chick* are from Down Under and feature some serious female surf action. *Australian Surfing Life* (ASL), *Tracks*, *Waves* and *In Deep* are the top Australian magazines and focus mainly on Aussie surfers, the world tour and travel. For longboarders a US publication, *Longboarder*, is available through some surf shops and certain newsagents.

But surfing isn't the only board sport out there – there's also skating and snowboarding to complete the full 'triple S' lifestyle – and you'd be amazed at how many surfers skateboard and snowboarders surf! So for a taste of the full boarding experience, *Adrenalin* magazine covers the lot including lifestyle elements. *Document* and *Sidewalk Surfer* are the UK's two top skateboard magazines, while for those of you who want to surf downhill on frozen water, there's *Snowboard UK*, *Whitelines*, *Onboard* and *Document Snow*.

Best of all, when you're done reading them you can cut them up and use them to decorate your books or paper your bedroom walls!

SURF READS

This book is just the tip of the iceberg. There are hundreds of great books out there, covering every aspect of surfing and surf culture.

History books don't have to just be about the Norman Conquest or the Lords and the 'serfs'. In Chapter 2 you had a brief glimpse of surfing's illustrious past, but if you want to know more, then there are plenty of books about the guys who invented and literally shaped surfing to keep you busy. Nat Young's *History of Surfing* takes you on a journey from the birth of surf through to modern day with some great photos to illustrate the ride. Nat was one of the guys who helped revolutionise the sport and was at the forefront of the shortboard movement at the end of the Sixties. And Nat Young's biography is called *Nat's Nat and That's That.* If you just can't get enough of interviews with your surf heroes, then *Above the Roar* is the book for you. Written by the former editor of top US mag, *Surfer*, it's bursting with fifty top interviews and great photos and illustrations.

A good book for anyone learning to surf is called *Caught Inside*, by Daniel Duane. Duane moves to the coast at Santa Cruz to learn to surf and his book follows his first year as he struggles to his feet both in and out of the water.

North Shore Chronicles by Bruce Jenkins is an adrenalin-packed read, uncovering the world of big-wave riders. Bruce spent a season on the North Shore of Hawaii, during which he was almost washed away while asleep in his room by a 'freak wave'. His book profiles some of big wave surfing's larger-than-life characters. In *Walking on Water* the British surf novice Andy Martin is also drawn to Hawaii's North Shore. The book highlights his adventures and the characters he meets on his search for the ultimate ride.

If you want to broaden your horizons, Low Pressure's *Stormrider* guides are a good starting point with maps and basic information on how the breaks work. Closer to home, *Surf UK* by Alf Alderson will guide you around 300 of the UK's surf spots.

From Indonesia to Australia, whatever your destination there's bound to be a book out there for you. Check out what www.amazon.co.uk has to offer.

But when it comes to surf exploration, nothing beats a good World Atlas. Break it open and just check out how many miles of coastline there are and let your mind wander!

What are the riders top reads?

Well, this is as mixed as their musical tastes. Some of them can't get enough of surfing, while others just need something to take their minds off their next competition heat.

Russ Winter – **'I'm in the middle of reading Harry Potter.'**

Sam Lamiroy – **'Bustin' Down the Door by Rabbit Bartholomew – Rabbit's the epitome of surfing culture. He was a brilliant surfer, he was the Kelly Slater of his day.'**

Sarah Bentley – **'Girl in the Curl – it's all about women's surfing, how it started and where it's heading. It's now one of the fastest growing sports for girls.'**

Eneko Acero – **'Nothing to do with surfing, just a good novel!'**

SURF ON THE WIDE SCREEN

From the latest new-skool vids to classic old-skool greats, these films can help lift your spirits on even the flattest weekend. Make sure you're watching carefully because there'll be a test at the end.

Cult films

These are the must-see backbone of surfing. The first is the most famous surf film of all time. *The Endless Summer* follows two surfers, Robert August and Mike Hynson, on a round-the-world surf trip in the days when going on holiday meant a trip to the next county. Filmed in the early Sixties by Bruce Brown, the pair started in the heart of Africa and rode waves never seen by surfers before. From here they travelled to South Africa and on to previously un-ridden Tahiti. In the days before video and DVD, films would show in local cinemas, surf films having a short run in coastal towns. *The Endless*

Summer was the first surf film ever to have a distribution across the whole of America. For today's surfers it is a must see, showing how far things have progressed. It is also great to listen to Brown's number-obsessed commentary. **'If you surf on an un-netted beach there's a 50/50 chance you'll be killed ... water temperature 70 degrees ... if you surfed all the beaches it would take you 100 years ... if you tread on a stonefish you'll die in 15 minutes.'** Classic. For a double billing, follow up with *Endless Summer 2* and see Pat O'Connel and Wingnut in another global adventure. Shot in the nineties by Bruce Brown, it highlights the revolution surfing has undergone in those thirty years.

Four-times World Champ Mark Richards' favourite cult film is one that comes up time and again: *Freeride*. **'I think is an incredible movie. The sound-track's great – it's one of those movies that has a place in history.'** This film, along with *Morning of the Earth*, *Evolution* and *Crystal Voyager*, shows an era in the late Sixties and early Seventies when surfing was undergoing a massive change and when surf exploration was exploding on to the screen. As Sarah Bentley sums up, **'In these films there was no anger, just healthy people going out surfing in bright clothes with great mellow music.'**

Hollywood surf

Next on the list has to be Hollywood's best attempt at a surf film, *Big Wednesday*. Set between 1962 and 1974 it follows three surf friends through the trials of growing up, the effects of the Vietnam war and their eventual reunion. The best film about surfing ever made. **'Big**

Wednesday is a classic,' says Gabe Davies. **'It was a real eye-opener when I was a little kid. It was and is still unbeaten for the surf footage.'**

Others to watch include *North Shore*, a film about a young surfer who learns to surf in a wave pool and hits the North Shore of Oahu looking for fame and fortune. Great to spot the top surfers playing characters in the film. Look out for Gerry Lopez, Occy, Robbie Page, Shaun Thompson, the Ho brothers and Laird Hamilton as the bad guy. Very cheesy and great fun. **'North Shore is a classic,'** says Fred Patacchia. **'I don't know if you can top that. Everyone knows at least three or four lines from that film.'**

Point Break and the UK's *Blue Juice* are average film attempts at capturing the surfing spirit but are worth a watch. While ones to avoid would have to include *In God's Hands*, a big Hollywood production which is only saved by some impressive tow-in action.

In terms of girls on film, *Gidget* was the movie that started the Sixties' surfing boom, telling the story of a young girl's adventures hanging out and surfing at Malibu. It is based on the writer's daughter's real life experiences, after she was nick-named Gidget by the Malibu surfers she befriended. More recently, the 2002 release of *Blue Crush* has caused a female surf rush in the States. A story of girl surfers on Hawaii's North Shore, the film features pro surfers **Megan Abubo** and **Rochelle Ballard** as themselves and doing stunt work alongside Layne Beachley, Keala Kenneley and **Kate Skarrat**. As Sarah Bentley says **'Blue Crush is really inspirational. It's an all-girl surfing** film showing waves from all over the world.'

Modern-day classics

Litmus is a modern old-skool masterpiece. If you want to know where surfing has come from and where it's going, this is a must. You can see great performances from the legendary Derek Hynd, Wayne Lynch and Tom Curren among others. You can also see a rare appearance of some of Ireland's top waves! Tiago Pires would recommend the film. **'My favourite surf film is *Litmus* because it has great footage and is slightly more mellow.'**

Searching for Tom Curren is a profile of one of surfing's living legends. A man of few words, Curren does his talking out in the line-up. Watch Curren ride J-Bay to see how a wave really should be ridden.

'*September Sessions*, that has to be my favourite film,' recalls Mark Richards. **'The music is incredible, the waves are phenomenal and the surfing is out of this world. It isn't like loud music and fast cuts – it's really quiet acoustic music and each wave goes from the start to the finish.'**

Momentum is another popular choice but the one that sits at the top of many surfers' film charts is *Shelter*. As Marlon Likpe says **'I liked *Shelter* a lot as it's a lot more than the usual guitar music and surfing; it has a bit more story to it.'** *Endless Summer 2* star Pat O'Connell simply says **'*Shelter* made me proud to be a surfer.'**

But for the newest releases and the latest new skool videos keep your eyes open and check out websites like **www.blackdiamond.co.uk**

SURF THE NET

To get an idea of just how huge surfing is, take a look around the Internet.

From the UK's and the world's top magazine sites to your favourite surf company, they all have a site. We couldn't possibly list them all but here are a few to get you started.

www.surfersvillage.com is a great place to get news from around the world of surfing.

www.aspworldtour.com is the ASP's official site and will keep you up to date with competition news and results.

www.aspeurope.com will let you know the latest European results and information.

www.quiksilver.com

www.billabong.com

www.oneill.com

www.rusty.com

www.ripcurl.com

www.lostenterprises.com

www.volcom.com and www.hurley.com

In fact most surf brands will have their own sites with rider profiles, action shots, news, downloads. etc. Check 'em out.

Environmental groups include:

www.sas.org.uk

www.surfrider.org

www.wdcs.org (Whale and Dolphin Conservation Soc) and www.mcsuk.org (Marine Conservation Soc)

Magazine sites include:

www.wahinemagazine.com is the US girls' mag, www.orca-surf.co.uk is the site for *Carve* magazine in the UK, while

www.surfermag.com and
www.surfingthemag.com are the two US mag sites.
Others to look at include:
www.coldwatersoul.co.uk for some great pics of breaks from
around the UK.
www.coldswell.com
www.surfmagic.co.uk is an e-zine with everything from
news to webcams.
www.swell.com US e-zine.
www.surflink.com e-zine is packed with news and stories
www.beachbeatsurfboards.co.uk all you wanted to know
about board design
www.surfhistory.com gives surfing's histories
www.bbc.co.uk/weather is indispensable for tracking those
lows.
www.britsurf.co.uk BSA website
www.britsurf.org is a listings and classifieds site for the UK

10
The pro files

'I think that everyone who goes through an era in surfing would like to think that their era is best, but each period in time is unique, as is each chapter in surfing history.' Mark Richards, four-times World Champion

Heroes, heroines and legends waiting in the wings...

Each era has its own heroes and heroines who have pushed back the boundaries of surfing. Whether they've changed the board we ride or how we ride it, they've all contributed to make surfing the unique lifestyle it is today. Looking to the future it's hard to envisage where the next Micky Dora or Simon Anderson is going to come from, but it'll happen, and surfing will continue to progress. Just as it's important to know wave riding's history, it's also important to know a few of the hands that are set to shape surfing's future.

Kelly Slater, USA

As leader of the new-skool revolution, when Kelly Slater stepped on to his surfboard, everything changed. At 21 he took his first World Title victory and went on to win an unprecedented further five times. The undisputed king of the waves stepped off the tour into semi-retirement following his win in 1998. Well, almost. He went on to redefine surfing's boundaries by merging 'new skool' moves with 'old skool' power surfing. As a grommet he was ribbed by his Hawaiian surf friends for his fear of big waves. As a man Slater has charged at some of the most respected big-wave spots on the planet, ultimately winning the most prestigious big-wave event, The Quiksilver In Memory of Eddie Aikau – only held when the waves are breaking over 20ft! Mark Richards, who has himself inspired a whole generation of surfers, describes Kelly as *the* standout. **'When I think about the number of world titles Kelly has won and the incredible performances he has put in from 2ft beach breaks to 15ft waves at Pipeline, it's hard to get past him as the most inspirational surfer that has ever emerged. He's probably *the* guy who has changed the perceptions of what surfing is all about.'** Not content with just being the world's greatest surfer, Slater has also dabbled in acting (as seen on *Baywatch*), played in a successful band with fellow surfers Rob Machado and Peter King, and is a hot golfer. Is there anything he can't do?

Laird Hamilton, Hawaii

An all round 'waterman', Laird connects with the ocean in every way he can. From surfing, windsurfing, and body-surfing to paddleboarding and speed-sailing he is always pushing back the boundaries. With friends and fellow big-wave riders Darrick Doerner and Buzzy Kerbox, he helped to introduce the concept of tow-in surfing. Using personal water crafts such as jet-skis, it is possible to be towed into waves too big and powerful to simply paddle into. Hamilton and his team have been working on another new concept – a hydrofoil.

Combining a board with foot straps and a big keel, he can hover above the surface of the water and may eventually ride open ocean swells island to island, where the waves have not yet broken. Watch this space.

Andy Irons, Hawaii

Having cut his teeth on the amateur circuit, Andy won the prestigious HIC Pipeline Pro in 1996 while still at school, knocking out many experienced big-league pros! Since 1997, he has leapfrogged between the WQS and WCT circuit, coming back hard in 2000 to beat Slater at Pipeline. 2002 was an awesome year for Irons seeing him win The Vans Triple Crown, Pipe Masters and ultimately the World Championship. From here the future looks very bright.

CJ Hobgood, USA

CJ and his twin brother Damien are goofy footed surf stars from Florida. From 1991 to 1997, they dominated most local and national competitions in their age group. Both are currently among the top riders on the WCT with CJ having claimed the 2001 World Title.

Cory Lopez, USA

As a new-skool free surfer and competitor, Cory's voice and style have helped change the criteria for judging contests, encouraging points to be awarded for innovation and progressive riding. With an all-round 'waterman' father and brother Shea a fellow competitor on the WCT, Cory was always heading for a life in the waves, but what he does when he gets there – aerials, snaps and radical manoeuvres – puts him in a class of his own.

Joel Tudor, USA and Bonga Perkins, Hawaii

A modern-day longboarding legend, riding his board with traditional old-skool style, Joel has been surfing competitively since he was just 14 and is partly responsible for the revival of longboarding. In 1998, aged just 22, he became the World Longboarding Champion and has continued to be outspoken in his views on modern longboarding.

Perkins is the new-skool longboarding whiz kid from Hawaii who believes that longboarding is about the equipment you use, not the way you ride it. He manages to put his stick into positions even some shortboarders would envy. These two riders are classic examples of tradition versus modernization.

Russell Winter, UK

Russell is Europe's hottest surfer. Having fought his way through the ultra-competitive WQS circuit, in 1998 Russell won one of the coveted few slots on the WCT. He overcame injury and lack of sponsorship to stay on the world tour for 2002 and was still the only European surfer since Martin Potter to qualify. Following a tough year, 2003 will see Russell drop down the ranks of WQS.

Others to watch out for on the WCT include **Taj Burrows**, **Mick Lowe**, **Mick Fanning**, **Joel Parkinson**, **Tim Curran** and **Nathan Hedge**.

Europe's finest
Eneko Acero, Euskadi

Eneko is one of Europe's most talented surfers and a

master tactician. The 2001 European Surfing Champion from the Basque region of Spain is already proving to be world class on the WQS and looks to be heading for the WCT. Hot on his heels is his younger brother Kepa.

Tiago Pires, Portugal

Portugal's Tiago is another European with the ability to perform at the highest level. He proved himself to be a top class performer, finishing as runner-up at the Rip Curl Sunset Pro in Hawaii's big waves in 2000. By the end of 2002 he was on the verge of the WCT.

The north east's Sam Lamiroy is a hard-working and charismatic surfer both in and out of the water. One of Europe's best-known surfers, Sam is currently working his way up the WQS ladder. Another regular on the qualifying circuit, Gabe Davies is one of the world's most famous free-surfers. The former English and British champion has covered virtually the whole globe in search of waves, earning him respect from surfing's elite.

Other up-and-coming surfers to look out for include Brits **Alan Stokes**, **Nathan Phillips**, **Shaun Skilton** and **Jake Boex.** Germany's **Marlon Lipke** and France's **Micky Picon**, **Fred Robin**, **Eric Rebiere** and **Patrick Beven** are also top Europeans going forward.

Women

Lisa Andersen, USA

She has undoubtedly pushed women's surfing into the limelight and challenged perceptions of female boardriding from the outset. As top British female surfer Sarah Bentley explains, **'Whenever you see a picture of Lisa Andersen she always looks so strong and powerful. It's a real inspiration.'** As a teenager, she was the only girl on her high school surf team. A few years later, aged 16, she bought a plane ticket to LA, leaving her mother a note in explanation, 'I'm leaving to become the world champion of women's surfing.' At 17 she turned pro, but it wasn't until after the birth of her baby daughter that in 1994 she won the first of four consecutive World Titles, only to be halted by a back injury. Lisa is a stand-out in the world of surfing and in 1995 she received the ultimate accolade of the cover shot for *Surfer* magazine. The caption was aimed at the mainly male readership and read 'Lisa Andersen surfs better than you.'

Layne Beachley, Australia

In 1998 Layne won her first world title and was photographed surfing a 30-ft tow-in wave with her partner, big-wave charger Ken Bradshaw. With five consecutive world titles under her belt and a passion for big-wave riding, Layne is the undisputed Queen of the waves.

Rochelle Ballard, Hawaii

Belle of the barrel, Rochelle has proved herself a talented tube rider but after more than ten years on the pro circuit she has yet to win a coveted world title.

Megan Abubo and **Keala Kennely** are the hottest new female surfers to come out of Hawaii. Having completed her first year on the tour in 2000, Keala charges herself with music to create explosive surfing whether busting new skool aerials or riding hard at Tahiti's death defying Teahupoo. Megan has proved herself both on the WCT with her strong manoeuvres and on film with a cameo role in the Hollywood surf flick *Blue Crush*. These are two strong contenders to follow as they rise up the WCT.

Brazil's **Jacqueline Silva** and Australian **Melanie Redman-Carr** are strong challengers for the world title. Other up and coming girls from Down Under include **Chelsea Georgeson**, and **Sam Cornish** – whose strong style is tipped to set the WCT alight.

In the European corner, 2003 sees France's **Marie-Pierre Abgrall** step on to the WCT, the first European female surfer ever to qualify. Top European WQS riders pushing up include France's **Emmanuelle Joly**, Spain's **Adelina Taylor** and the UK's top competitive female surfer **Robyn Davies**. Other Brits to watch include **Tracy Boxall**, **Sarah Whiteley** and **Sarah Bentley**, the 2002 Cornish Open Champion. Sarah Bentley is also one of the UK's top free surfers and is at home in waves as far afield as Australia, Mexico or at her local break St Agnes.

11
Surf comps

SO YOU WANT TO BE A SURF STAR ...

So you've got the poster up on your wall – one of the top surfers on a perfect wave in a tropical paradise. But how do they get this awesome lifestyle and could that be you in a few years' time?

Surfing has always had a competitive edge to it, whether it is competing with yourself or trying to be the best surfer at your break. Competition is a great way to improve your surfing, meet new friends and see new places. But if you want to follow Russell Winter on to the World Tour, where do you start?

'I started surfing in contests when I was about 10 or 11,' says Australian surfer and four-times World Champion Mark Richards. **'In Newcastle there was a schoolboy's event each year. I just started surfing and winning trophies. I thought "cool, get a big trophy" – they were pretty ugly, but at the time it was awesome. It just developed from there into the Cadets – under-16, into the Juniors – under-18, and then into the seniors which was over-18. It was sort of like one day we were getting trophies and the next day people were sticking cheques in our hands.'**

Local surf competitions are where the world's best

surfers started out, from Kelly Slater and Lisa Andersen to surfing's next superstars like CJ Hobgood. Local comps will teach you how competitions run and how to compete. **'If you have any interest in really developing your surfing, then go and do any contest you can. It's all experience,'** advises top European surfer Sam Lamiroy from Newcastle. **'It may send you into a crumpled heap of misery with every heat that you lose – because you will lose heats on the way to success – but you learn from every one. It's not only about natural talent.'**

How do you win a surf competition?

All the surfers in any surf competition go through a series of knock-out heats. Successful surfers progress to a heat in the next round until they are knocked out or reach the final. It works the same way as the FA Cup. Riders are either in heats with three other surfers, in which case the top two qualify, or in heats with one other, in which case the winner progresses. Local and national events usually take place over one or two days with heats usually lasting about 15 to 20 minutes.

But how do you win your heat? Well, as the top BSA coach explains, preparation is the key. **'Make sure you have the right equipment and things like a spare leash, block of wax and your wetsuit! It's all about good preparation.'**

Competitors are scored on the manoeuvres they perform on a wave. Some manoeuvres are more difficult and are scored more highly, as are moves nearer the steepest part of the wave, close to the curl. Surfers' scores for their best three or four waves are added up at the end of the heat.

Familiarise yourself with the rule book and brush up on what the judges are looking for. As Barrie sums up, **'Practise, prepare and know the rules. Other than that just concentrate on doing what you are capable of. If it's enough, you'll win first place, if not you'll know that you went out there and gave it your best. Just focus on enjoying it.'**

But competition might not be for everyone. It can be a nerve-wracking experience as top women's surfer Sarah Bentley found out. **'My first competition was in Newquay and I got through the first round and then when my second heat was coming up I went and had a cup of tea and some breakfast and purposely missed my heat. I didn't feel worthy enough to go into the second round to compete. I felt really inadequate, like I shouldn't be there.'**

What is a professional surfer?

When Lisa Andersen started competing, it was the trophies and thrill of the winning that kept her going. **'I think I started competing because I began to get good at it and people talked of "potential" and saying that I should compete,'** remembers Lisa. **'I didn't really know I wanted to be a professional surfer or that there was such a thing as a professional circuit at the time.'**

You will hear the term 'professional' surfer a lot. But what is a professional, and how does he or she become one? It's somebody who surfs for a living, supported by at least one sponsor who pays the rider and/or helps with their expenses for travel, accommodation and equipment. **'It's a two-way relationship,'** explains Sam Lamiroy. **'The flip side of the coin is that you are somebody who wears and endorses that product and through you they can associate their brand with the surfing lifestyle and the surfing image. The better you are at being a billboard or a microphone for their product, the more they will reward you. It is a business. Very few companies out there are charities. You get back what you put in.'**

How to approach sponsors

'Keep your head down and improve your surfing to a reasonable standard – don't expect to be able to get a sponsor if you can stand up and go along a wave. Then do some local or national contests in your age divisions,' explains Sam Lamiroy. **'If you get your picture in a magazine or local paper, save it. Put a little package together – even if you don't have a published picture of you surfing, just get a decent picture of yourself and send it off.'**

'Pitch yourself right – understand a little bit about what they're after. Go for brands that you like and don't go expecting £10,000. Ask for product and maybe a little photo incentive package so if you get your picture in the magazines you'll receive some money. Then if you improve, that's the time to speak to other top surfers in the country to see what sort of packages they are on, because it's difficult to

know how much you are worth as a professional surfer.'

As European champion Eneko Acero points out, when you're young you shouldn't worry too much about chasing sponsors. **'When we were young we just competed in contests and if you did very well everyone would know. So we'd just compete for fun and people would come up to us at the contest and talk about sponsorship.'** It seems to have paid off for Eneko, who has equipment and clothing sponsors as well as being paid so he can concentrate on his surfing and working his way on to the WCT.

TRICKS OF THE TRADE – HOW TO WIN

Marlon Lipke is a surfer on the tough WQS tour. The German rider has the following advice for up-and-coming surfers: **'Don't do stupid moves on the wave – be patient, get speed and do bigger moves. Do proper turns – decent bottom turns, really push it.'**

'If you get a good first manoeuvre going you'll get a good wave,' says Fred Patacchia.

Lisa Andersen stays focused and hungry for her next wave. **'Not everywhere we go is perfect. Some waves aren't that good, but you're hungry to surf better waves – so when you do, you're so into it you do well!'**

Tour veteran Pat O'Connell believes in taking it one step at a time. **'Surfing can be extremely frustrating – you're dealing with a changing environment and it takes time to figure it out.'** Top French surfer and former European champion Micky Picon echoes this. **'My advice would be to surf a lot more – it helps you to learn about the ocean and about waves.'** Ex-British and English champion Gabe Davies agrees. **'Get as much time in the water as possible. To get to the top you'll have to start competing pretty young, but really, time in the water is the only way to do it.'**

'Sunny Garcia gave me some really good advice,' says Kelly Slater. **'If something goes wrong don't blame others – look at yourself. Most often you can find an answer in yourself.'**

This advice is echoed by fellow WCT surfer Damien Hobgood who says, **'My dad always tried to tell us just to have fun and enjoy ourselves and if we didn't do well that it didn't really matter. It's easy to get caught up in the competition and everything. I just try to remember that surfing is a blessing and should be fun!'**

Sam Lamiroy's advice is **'Don't take anything for granted because it's an amazing thing to be able to do. I think it's one of those things that you'll look back on one day and think *I was actually pretty good.'***

ASP WORLD CHAMPIONSHIP TOUR AND WORLD QUALIFYING TOUR

The World Championship Tour (WCT) is the Premier League of world surfing. Only 44 surfers can compete on the men's tour and 15 on the women's tour, so competition for these places is extremely fierce. Russell Winter was the only European on the 2002 WCT. What gives him the biggest buzz is **'getting to surf good**

waves at spots like J-Bay and getting drawn against the top surfers in the world. The feeling that you get – trying to beat guys like Kelly Slater, when there are just two of you surfing an amazing break like Jeffrey's Bay – is just incredible. I love it.'

The WCT works in the same way as the motor racing grand prix circuit. There are a number of events around the world at some of the planet's best surfing locations and at the end of the year a world champion is crowned.

But how do you get on to the WCT with its lucrative sponsorship contracts and superstar status? Well each year a number of surfers are relegated from the tour, and the best surfers on the World Qualifying Series are promoted. The WQS is like the WCT in that there are a number of events throughout the year with points available towards qualification. The better a surfer does, the more points they accumulate. As Russell Winter explains, stepping up to the WQS from national events is a big step. **'WQS contests are much harder than national and European events. Surfers from all over the world are competing – Brazil, Australia, America, Hawaii, and they're all good surfers – young guys too. Then the WCT is another big step up again.'**

But it's not all perfect waves and exotic locations. Life on the road can be hard with surfers seeing home for only a few weeks in the year. As Lisa Andersen explains, sometimes the pleasure of being in foreign lands can wear off. **'After thirteen years of living out of a bag, yes, it can wear off. I've**

not worn every item in my closet for years because I only travel with certain clothes, and just repack them.'

Russell Winter agrees. **'You have to spend a lot of time away from home, and that's what I miss – just coming home to Newquay for a couple of weeks. If you want to do it as a career, it will be like that from your early twenties through to your thirties. That's a long time to spend away, but you get used to it.'**

ANNUAL COMPETITIONS

So you've got a pretty good cut back and you've been practising your 'off the lip'. Why not get down to your local contest and show what you can do? You may even win yourself some cool gear! In the UK there are about 35 BSA-recognized contests, catering for surfers from grommets to seniors and longboarders to short-boarders. The line-up is likely to alter every year, and events may even be cancelled due to bad conditions; so for up-to-date listings, check out the British Surfing Association website: www.britsurf.co.uk. As well as local events there are big national contests including the English National Championships, the Welsh National Championships, the British National Championships, the British Cup, the Channel Islands Junior Championships and the Newquay Surf Festival.

Moving up from the national events is the European Professional Surfing Association (EPSA) tour. Running from March to November, currently the men's tour holds about 10 events and the women's just 2. Selected WQS 1–3 star events in Spain, Portugal, France and the Canaries are used to compete for EPSA points, so as

2001 European Champion Eneko Acero points out, **'The EPSA is a good place to gain the experience needed for the next step up to the WQS.'**

Due to the large number of surfers competing, there are about 50 men's and 15 women's WQS events held across the world from Hawaii to Europe. Probably the best event to check out, and the easiest to get to, is our very own 4-star-rated Rip Curl Newquay Pro. Won in 2002 by Cornwall's Russell Winter, the Newquay event, held in July/August, attracts big-name competitors from across the globe and is a good place to spot surfing's rising stars.

The competitors on the WCT travel from March until December, competing in about 12 contests for the men and 6 for the women. Then they go on to Europe for September and October, surfing in Portugal, the south west coast of France and Basque Spain. Both the men and the women finish up for a winter in Hawaii.

You may have seen the pros busting their moves on videos, but there's nothing like seeing them in the flesh. It's the difference between seeing the football highlights and sitting on the touchline at the big game. The breaks around the contest site will also be packed with the world's best riders warming up before their heats. This makes the sport unique as you can paddle out and share a peak with your heroes – a session you'll never forget! Just ask a soccer fan what they'd give to have a kickaround with David Beckham before a Man U game or a golfer how they'd feel having a round with Tiger Woods before a tournament. The contest site also makes the riders accessible and all the guys and girls on the tour are more than happy to sign a few autographs and even pass on a few tips, so what are you waiting for?

As with the national contests, all events are liable to change, but you can keep up to date with what's happening on the contest scene – from EPSA to WCT – at the ASP website: www.aspeurope.com and check out how the pros are getting on at www.aspworldtour.com.

Ultimately, it's not about the prizes and the logos. Surfing's all about the stoke – sharing the waves with your mates and the stories afterwards. It's something that will stay with you forever. Hopefully, this book has inspired you to get out there and catch your first wave. Nothing will beat that feeling of your first ride, except the next and the next and the next; and who knows, maybe you'll end up being that surfer on the poster, tearing it up in a tropical paradise. Just keep your eye on the chart ...

12
Glossary

Cracking the surf code, the A–Z of surf lingo …

A

Aerial – Skateboard-inspired move where a surfer launches up the face of the wave on their board and into the air before landing back on the wave.

B

Backhand – A surfer riding with their back to the wave.

Banana boards – A board with a lot of nose and tail 'rocker', said jokingly to resemble a banana in profile. Surfed by Slater in early Nineties.

Barrel – A hollow wave where the lip throws over forming a tunnel. Also used to describe riding in the tube.

Biodegradable – A substance that is broken down when it is introduced into the environment, for example waste food or paper. Non-biodegradable is a substance that will not break down when introduced into the environment, for example plastic.

Bottom turn – An arcing turn that takes a surfer from the drop on to the open face or into their first manoeuvre.

Burned – Surfer dropped-in on has been burned.

BSA – British Surfing Association.

C

Carve – Classic turn on the open face with the rail buried.

Channels – A rip used by surfers to get out to the line up. Also used to describe a series of long, thin, straight depressions carved into the bottom of the board near the tail which affect the way the board handles.

Charging – Surfing hard.

Close-out – When the whole length of a wave breaks at once.

Concave – The bottom contour of a board where the shaper has taken more material out of the middle of the board than at the rails giving a concave profile when looked at in cross section from the front.

Curl – The steepest part of the wave next to where it is breaking. Area that generates greatest speed for the surfer.

Cutback – Turning back from the open face into the pocket near the curl.

D

Dawn patrol – Getting up for an early morning surf session.

Deck – The top of the board where the surfer stands.

Deck grip – A self-adhesive spongy mat which is stuck to the deck of a surfboard to provide a grippy surface to stand on.

Dings – Depressions and punctures in a surfboard.

Drop-in – To take off on another surfer's wave.

Drop knee turn – When a surfer stands on the back of the board, drops their back knee and cranks the board into a turn with the nose out of the water. Classic old skool manoeuvre.

Duck-dive – A way of getting you and your board under waves and out into the line-up.

F

Fins – Curved fibreglass fixed rudders under the tail of the surfboard, which help the board to turn when the surfer leans.

Fish – A short, wide surfboard with a swallow tail designed for small waves.

Floater – When a surfer rides up the wave, along the top and drops back on to the face.

Frontside – A surfer riding facing the wave.

G

Glassing – The process of applying fibreglass and resin to a surfboard.

Glassy – Smooth, perfect waves. Also morning glass.

Gnarly – Used to describe a dangerous or big wave.

Goofy footer – A surfer who surfs with their right foot forward.

Going off – When the surf is epic or when someone is surfing really well.

Green room – Riding inside a tube.

Grommet – Young surfer.

Groynes – Wooden fence sunk into the beach to stop sand being washed away.

Gun – A long stretched thruster used for riding big waves. Usually between 7'6' and 9ft long.

H

Hang Ten – When a surfer stands on the nose of a longboard with all their toes over the front edge of the board.

I

Inside – The area inside where the waves are breaking.

In the slot – If a low pressure is in the right place to send swell on to a stretch of coastline.

K

Kook – Surfer without a clue.

L

Leash – Elasticated cord that secures the surfboard to the surfer and prevents the board being lost when the surfer wipes out.

Lip – The pitching part of the wave.

Longboards – Boards over 9ft with one or three fins and a rounded nose.

Low pressure – A spinning weather system that draws in air and causes swell to be generated.

M

Malibu or **Mal** – Traditional-style longboard with one fin.

Mini-gun – A long, thin thruster between 7 and 8ft long designed for bigger surf.

Mini-mal – A wide, round-nosed surfboard between 7 and 8ft long.

N

New skool – When a new style of surfing or dressing comes along it is often called new skool.

North Shore – The North Shore of the Hawaiian island of Oahu. Also a cult film.

Nose – The front end of the board.

Noseguard/nosecone – Covers the sharp nose of a surfboard with a rubbery cover to help prevent any injuries.

O

Offshore – Wind blowing off the land and out to sea. Helps produce better quality, clean waves.

Old skool – Something which is traditional, such as a traditional way of dressing or a traditional way of riding a surfboard.

Onshore – Wind blowing from the sea on to the land. Causes poor quality waves that crumble into white water.

P

Peak – A wave that breaks both left and right from one point. It is also used to describe the part of the line up where the wave breaks first.

Pearling – To catch a rail and fall off.

Peel – A rideable wave breaking smoothly from the peak through to the inside without closing out.

Point – A finger of land along which waves break.

Pop / popping up – The motion of moving from lying prone to standing on the board.

Prone – Lying flat on the board.

Pull-out – When a surfer rides up the face of the wave and exits off the back.

R

Rails – The edges of the board.

Reef – An area of raised rocks, coral or boulders upon which waves break.

Regular footer – A surfer who stands on their board with their left foot forward.

Rips – Currents of water moving along or away from the beach.

Ripping – Surfing like a superstar. A ripper!

S

Sandbar – A bottom contour made up of raised sand upon which waves break.

Set waves – Waves that are slightly bigger than the average waves in a swell, arrive in groups called a set.

Shaper – A person who shapes surfboards.

Shortboards – Boards under 7ft with a pointed nose and usually three fins.

Shortie – A wetsuit with short sleeves and short legs.

Shoulder – The unbroken part of the wave away from the peak where the wave is not very steep.

Shredding – Surfing like a pro.

Sick – A wave or a ride that was amazing.

Single fin – A surfboard with only one fin.

Slash – A turn at the top of the wave where the tail throws a lot of spray.

Snake – To paddle round a surfer who has priority and to steal their wave.

Snap in the pocket – manoeuvre where a surfer heads vertically up the face of the wave and turns sharply under the lip where the wave is breaking.

Soul surfer – Surfer who rides for the stoke, not the cash.

Sponsor – A company that backs a surfer with either money or products in return for exposure in the media.

Spring suit – A wetsuit with long legs and short sleeves.

Steamer – A wetsuit with long sleeves and long legs.

Stoked – More than happy, i.e. 'Totally stoked I pulled off that floater!'

Stringer – The centre line of the board which is made of wood and gives the board extra strength.

Surf camp – A place providing accommodation, sometimes with tuition, by the coast.

Surfed out – Tired after an epic session shredding the blue.

Surf school – An organization or company that provides tuition and usually equipment needed to learn to surf.

Swell – Generated by the wind blowing on the surface of the ocean, swell is made up of peaks and troughs travelling away from the low pressure that generated it, with the peaks breaking as waves when they hit land.

T

Tail – The back of the surfboard.

Tail slide – A turn high on the face where the tail breaks free and is pushed around, throwing spray.

Three sixty – A manoeuvre in which a surfer and their board turns through 360° and carries on surfing.

Thruster – A short surfboard with three fins and a pointed nose.

Tides – The cycle of water movement caused by the pull of the moon.

Tow-in – The use of jet skis to tow surfers into waves, usually at big wave spots.

Trimming – When a surfer sets the rail in the face of the wave and rides diagonally along the wave, gathering speed from the forward motion of the wave.

Tube ride – Riding in a hollow wave.

Twin fin – A short surfboard with two fins.

Walk the board – Old-skool move where a surfer walks along the board towards the nose and back.

Wall – Steep part of the wave that hasn't yet broken.

Waterman – Used to describe a person who spends a lot of time in the water not just surfing but windsurfing, kite-surfing, swimming, lifeguarding and paddleboarding.

Wax – Rubbed on to the deck of a surfboard to provide a grippy surface to stand on.

WCT – The World Championship Tour of surfing is the sports competitive top flight.

Wetsuit – A neoprene all-in-one suit designed to keep a surfer warm in the water.

White water – The turbulent inside part of the wave that has broken and is rolling towards the beach.

WQS – The World Qualifying Series is a series of competitions around the world that decides which surfers will qualify for the WCT.